Weeke & Short Breaks in Britain

- Including Haunted Hotels supplement
- Accommodation for holidays and weekends away

The harbour at Lynmouth, Devon   Photo courtesy of Rising Sun Hotel & Restaurant, Lynmouth

Foreword

The dreadful summer weather has left many of us feeling a little depressed and in need of a stress-busting boost, so a city or country break could be just the thing to perk us up. In this edition of **Weekend and Short Break Holidays** there is an excellent choice of accommodation, ranging from large and small hotels to B&Bs, and cosy, friendly guest houses and farmhouses, as well as self-catering properties and caravan parks, all offering the chance to enjoy that much needed break.

Anne Cuthbertson,
Editor

© FHG Guides Ltd, 2009
ISBN 978-1-85055-408-0

Maps: ©MAPS IN MINUTES™ / Collins Bartholomew 2007

Typeset by FHG Guides Ltd, Paisley.
Printed and bound in China by Imago.

Distribution. Book Trade: ORCA Book Services, Stanley House,
3 Fleets Lane, Poole, Dorset BH15 3AJ
(Tel: 01202 665432; Fax: 01202 666219)
e-mail: mail@orcabookservices.co.uk
Published by FHG Guides Ltd., Abbey Mill Business Centre,
Seedhill, Paisley PA1 ITJ (Tel: 0141-887 0428; Fax: 0141-889 7204).
e-mail: admin@fhguides.co.uk

Weekend & Short Breaks in Britain is published by FHG Guides Ltd,
part of Kuperard Group.

Cover design: FHG Guides
Cover Pictures: courtesy of Milkbere Cottage Holidays, Seaton, Devon.

Contents

Ratings & Awards

For the first time ever the AA, VisitBritain, VisitScotland, and the Wales Tourist Board will use a single method of assessing and rating serviced accommodation. Irrespective of which organisation inspects an establishment the rating awarded will be the same, using a common set of standards, giving a clear guide of what to expect. The RAC is no longer operating an Hotel inspection and accreditation business.

Accommodation Standards: Star Grading Scheme

Using a scale of 1-5 stars the objective quality ratings give a clear indication of accommodation standard, cleanliness, ambience, hospitality, service and food, This shows the full range of standards suitable for every budget and preference, and allows visitors to distinguish between the quality of accommodation and facilities on offer in different establishments. All types of board and self-catering accommodation are covered, including hotels, B&Bs, holiday parks, campus accommodation, hostels, caravans and camping, and boats.

VisitBritain and the regional tourist boards, enjoyEngland.com, VisitScotland and VisitWales, and the AA have full details of the grading system on their websites

The more stars, the higher level of quality

★★★★★
exceptional quality, with a degree of luxury

★★★★
excellent standard throughout

★★★
very good level of quality and comfort

★★
good quality, well presented and well run

★
acceptable quality; simple, practical, no frills

National Accessible Scheme

If you have particular mobility, visual or hearing needs, look out for the National Accessible Scheme. You can be confident of finding accommodation or attractions that meet your needs by looking for the following symbols.

 Typically suitable for a person with sufficient mobility to climb a flight of steps but would benefit from fixtures and fittings to aid balance

 Typically suitable for a person with restricted walking ability and for those that may need to use a wheelchair some of the time and can negotiate a maximum of three steps

 Typically suitable for a person who depends on the use of a wheelchair and transfers unaided to and from the wheelchair in a seated position. This person may be an independent traveller

 Typically suitable for a person who depends on the use of a wheelchair in a seated position. This person also requires personal or mechanical assistance (eg carer, hoist).

hauntedhotelguide.com

or True Believers or Open-minded Sceptics, this supplement gives you the opportunity to visit som of the Most Haunted Hotels in the Country.

Experience the Unexplained!

hauntedhotelguide.com was developed in late 2005 in response to the overwhelming demand for a definitive directory of haunted accommodation throughout the UK. With the public's interest in all things paranormal constantly growing, and with increasingly popular TV shows like *"Most Haunted"*, *"Dead Famous"* and *"Derek Acorah's Ghost Towns"* every hotel seems to have a ghost or two to boast about.

Whether you are a hardcore ghost fan or open-minded sceptic, **hauntedhotelguide.com** will provide you with invaluable haunted history about the ghostly goings-on at each hotel, along with the usual information you would expect to find from a regular hotel guide. With around 500 haunted hotels throughout the country, it should be easy to find the perfect location for your stay.

Whilst many other hotel guides concentrate on facilities provided, often the really interesting things, such as where to find the ghost of a servant girl in the Station Hotel or where the bones of the 'Blue Boy' of Chillingham Castle were discovered, are overlooked… Not by us… As you'd expect, we positively encourage reports such as these as we believe that the haunted history of a hotel is just as important as its facilities and we feel that the possibility of seeing a ghost tends to remain etched in your mind much longer than the amount of sherry you received on the welcome tray!

With detailed descriptions and images of the Haunted Hotels and Haunted Inns in this supplement and on our site, **hauntedhotelguide.com** is totally unique: Discover the Green Lady of Comlongon Castle; investigate the presence of a spectral monk in the Tansy Room at Hazlewood Castle, or try and spot the Ghostly Lady Jane in Dalston Hall.

Many of our hotels have been investigated by our Mediums, psychics and paranormal investigators. James Griffiths *(Derek Acorah's Ghost Towns)*, one of our mediums, has certainly had a few 'interesting' experiences to say the least:

'Having had the opportunity to visit some of the most haunted hotels throughout the UK, I can honestly say that they do live up to expectations! Being rather rudely pulled out of bed at the dead of night by the poisoned spectre of a lady does leave you wondering whether you will be charged extra for it in the morning as you were sure it wasn't mentioned in the brochure… Finding yourself confronted by a sword-wielding soldier within a castle gate house with only a torch and your mobile phone to defend yourself makes you question your decision to venture out on Halloween! And investigating a hotel in a village renowned for at least 12 ghosts, wondering which one they are all staying at and praying it's not yours, make's you realise there truly is another world waiting to be discovered…'

James Griffiths

If you want to find out to find out more about the hotels in this supplement or if you want to discover a haunted hotel near you, take a look at **hauntedhotelguide.com.**

We hope you enjoy the guide and may all your experiences be unexplainable…

Flitwick Manor

Church Road , Flitwick
Bedfordshire MK45 1AE
Tel: 01525 712242
Email : flitwick@menzieshotels.co.uk
www.menzies-hotels.co.uk

The luxurious **Flitwick Manor** is a Georgian gem. If you are fortunate enough, you may witness the ghost of an ex-housekeeper who is said to haunt the corridors...

Nestling in the tranquillity of acres of rolling gardens and wooded parkland, Flitwick Manor is a luxury hotel in the South East of England. This country house hotel, located near Woburn, is a classical Georgian house that continues its ancestral traditions of hospitality.

The cosy lounge of Flitwick Manor is elegantly furnished, providing the perfect retreat for those seeking peace and relaxation.

For private functions or business meetings, this country house hotel offers the ultimate in luxury in the South East, all just one hour from the centre of London.

With two AA rosettes, the restaurant at this luxury hotel is rated as one of the finest in the country and offers the ideal combination of fine dining in a delightful setting.

The 17 individually designed guestrooms and suites, furnished with fine antiques and period pieces, blend effortlessly together to offer guests a comfortable and endearing stay. If you're looking for a luxury hotel in the South East, look no further than Flitwick Manor.

HOTEL FEATURES

- 24 hour room service
- Award-winning restaurant
- Drawing room
- Gardens and woodlands
- Tennis Court • Croquet Lawn
- Helicopter landing pad

Haunted History

hauntedhotelguide
.com

Flitwick Manor is reputedly haunted by an ex-housekeeper who, over 100 years ago, was dismissed for allegedly poisoning one of the Lyall family, the former owners of the Manor. After the Old Housekeeper (whose proper name no-one knows) died, it seems her spirit decided to take up residence again at Flitwick.

She keeps herself to herself and doesn't stray much from the bedroom she has made her own. Staff at Flitwick Manor know the housekeeper's favourite chair - she even leaves an impression in the seat after sitting down!

Whilst building work was being carried out on Flitwick Manor, a concealed room was discovered behind some panelling. It has been suggested that this could have been the housekeeper's quarters. Ever since then the spirit has been making herself known to guests throughout the hotel. One guest was woken to find her sitting on the end of his bed, and a duty manager witnessed the ghost in one of the corridors...

stunning 16th Century **Lion and Swan Inn** in Congleton is steeped in
ory... A dark haired female spirit said to have lived during the Middle Ages
en makes an appearance...
ated at the heart of the attractive market town of Congleton, the strikingly
bered Lion and Swan Hotel is a traditional coaching inn which boasts 21
ractive bedrooms with every modern amenity, a first class restaurant which
des itself on a high standard of cuisine, and a friendly bar which is open to
idents and non residents alike featuring a wide selection of real ales, lagers,
es & spirits..
r restaurant, open for Breakfast, Lunch and Dinner seven days a week,
ves an eclectic selection of dishes freshly prepared in house using locally
urced fresh ingredients. The fireplace in the restaurant is a particular delight
d source of mystery with its complex and intriguing carvings...

Lion & Swan Hotel

Swan Bank, Congleton,
Cheshire
Tel: 01260 273 115
Email: info@lionandswan.co.uk
www.lionandswan.co.uk

HOTEL FEATURES
- Remote Control Colour Television
- AM/FM radio alarm clock
- Hairdryer • Ironing Facilities
- Full tea and coffee
making facilities.

aunted History   hauntedhotelguide.com

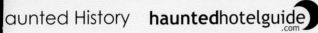

e carvings on the fireplace are often interpreted as demonic symbolism.
is may have something to do with the **Lion and Swan's** ghost - a young,
own haired woman, who often appears around a new moon, wearing
othing but a pair of clogs and a smile!
is young spirit reputedly dates back to the Middle Ages. It is alleged that she
as unable to conceive and drank a potion to aid conception. However,
stead of creating new life, the potion took hers. She has been seen on many
ccasions tending the fire beneath the carved fireplace...
e Tudor Suite is also renowned for its mysterious goings on. It sometimes has
cold atmosphere, and most of the unexplained noises emanate from here
t night.

he **George and Dragon Hotel** in Chester is an imposing building situated just
utside the city walls. As Chester is one of the most haunted cities in the UK, it
no surprise that this hotel has its own ghosts as guests...
short walk from Chester City centre, the George and Dragon is a traditional
ostelry that blends well with a modern lively bar. Our open plan lounge, with
hree fireplaces, creates a warm and cosy atmosphere to enjoy our well
tocked cellar and traditional food. The character building which now stands
n the site is around 100 years old, but there has been a public house or
coaching inn, of some kind, on the site for a lot longer.
There is also believed to be a burial ground of Roman origin on the site, which
s possible given that Chester, or Dewa was an important Roman town.

George & Dragon

1 Liverpool Road
Chester, Cheshire CH2 1AA
Tel: 01244 380714
Email : 7783@greeneking.co.uk
www.oldenglishinns.co.uk

HOTEL FEATURES
- Hairdryer
- Iron & Ironing Board
- Tea/Coffee • TV
- All en suite with shower room

Haunted History   hauntedhotelguide.com

Chester boasts over 2000 years of documented history. Its crypts, narrow
streets and alley ways play host to many infamous ghosts and spirits and the
George and Dragon Hotel is no exception. This hotel is reputedly haunted by
a legion of Roman soldiers.
The George and Dragon is situated on the site of the old Roman road leading
out from Chester. Roman military law forbade the burial of soldiers within the
city walls of Dewa and so many were buried immediately outside and some
could quite feasibly be buried beneath the hotel.
Over the centuries the sound of marching feet beneath the floors has been
heard by staff and guests alike. Strangely, the sound seems loudest in the
cellars, which would have been closer to the original Roman ground level...

Dalston Hall is a luxurious 15th Century Mansion with a fascinating history. La
Jane is said to appear in Tudor dress in the gallery above the manorial hall.
Other ghosts include a Handyman, 'Sad Emily' and a Young Girl...
Guests can expect a venue with a difference, and as witnessed by the GM
'Haunted' team, a few ghosts! The hotel offers a peaceful and tranquil sett
to guests, and the perfect retreat in the beautiful countryside on the northe
edge of the Lake District, ideally placed for the national treasure Hadrian's
Wall.
The hotel has recently undergone considerable refurbishment involving the
ground floor public areas being restyled but still keeping the original
character of this 15th Century family Mansion. The bedrooms have also bee
restyled to an elegant character but each has their own unique luxurious
style.

Dalston Hall

Carlisle
Cumbria CA5 7JX
Tel: +44 (0)1228 710271
Email: enquiries@dalstonhall.com
www.dalston-hall-hotel.co.uk

HOTEL FEATURES

- En suite bathroom
- Tea & Coffee making facilities
- TV • Award Winning Restaurant
- Wedding Licence
- Conference Facilities

Haunted History   **haunted**hotelguide
.com

Dalston Hall plays host to many ghosts, the first of which, the spirit of a
Victorian handyman, has been seen wandering the grounds. In the Baronia
Hall you may find Dalston Hall's oldest ghost – known to the staff as Lady
Jane. She appears in Tudor dress and may well be a member of one of the
Dalston families who owned the Hall for such a long time.
The cellars of the hotel are haunted by the sinister Mr Fingernails and many of
the bedrooms are reputed to have spectral guests: Room 4 is said to be
haunted by a poor maid who threw herself from the Pele tower and in Room
12 guests have complained of being woken by girls' voices whispering...

Set in 18 acres, **Walworth Castle** is one of the country 's finest historic hotels,
parts of which date back to the 12th century
Walworth Castle Hotel just outside Darlington in County Durham, was built in
1189 and is one of the few castle hotels in England. Recently refurbished to a
extremely high standard by owners Rachel and Chris Swain, Walworth Castle
Hotel really is the ideal venue to sample England's Living History
Each of the 34 bedrooms and numerous reception rooms has its own
particular character many with individually designed upholstery. The feature
rooms have been recently refurbished to an extremely high standard
Walworth Castle boasts two fabulous restaurants (one award-winning) and a
traditional 'pub'. The choice of hospitality at Walworth Castle Hotel really is
second to none.

Walworth Castle

Walworth, Darlington
Durham DL2 2LY
Tel: +44 (0)1325 485470
Email:
enquiries@walworthcastle.co.uk
www.walworthcastle.co.uk

HOTEL FEATURES

- Four-Poster Beds
- Sumptuous Furnishings
- Castle Gardens
- Fabulous Views
- TV

Haunted History   **haunted**hotelguide
.com

According to legend, the Lord of the Manor was having an affair with one of
the servant girls. Unfortunately, for both parties, the maid fell pregnant.
Realising that it would be a great disgrace to his family to father a child with a
servant he decided to take drastic action. At the time of the affair, the castle
was being renovated so the Lord of the Manor decided to seize the
opportunity and had the maid walled up inside a spiral staircase.
It is alleged that she can still be heard climbing the staircase behind the
library leading to the turrets of **Walworth Castle**
Other ghostly apparitions at the castle include the spectral replay of a
brother's feud resulting in one killing the other, the horse buried in the gardens,
and the running boy in the corridors...

e stunningly beautiful Redworth Hall dates back to
4. Redworth was the site of many battles during the
il War and it appears that some of the soldiers killed
attle are still lingering...
dworth Hall Hotel is a breathtaking Jacobean
untry house in County Durham. You'll feel as if you're
he middle of nowhere here as you survey the
ptivating, landscaped gardens and enchanting
odland. From the moment you sweep up the long
veway to the hotel, you know you're in for a treat.
u can enjoy the escapism of this picture postcard
tting and within 5 minutes be heading towards
ewcastle, historic Durham or York.
is original building still retains many of its original
atures including an ornate staircase, the Great Hall
d several four-poster bedrooms. The Hall also boasts
o award winning restaurants and a leisure club.
side from the hotel itself, you'll find it's the charm and
ospitality of north-east folk at Redworth Hall that will
ake your stay an incredible one.

Redworth Hall
Redworth,
Durham DL5 6NL
Tel: +44 (0)1388 770 600
Email:
redworthhall@paramount-hotels.co.uk
www.paramount-redworthhall.co.uk

HOTEL FEATURES
- Concierge
- Currency exchange
- Safety Deposit Boxes
- Restaurant
- Lounge / Bar
- Barber / Beauty Services

Haunted History   **haunted**hotelguide

Redworth Hall has a fantastic haunted history and boasts at least two ghosts...
The first is that of a woman who, it appears, felt the urge to throw herself from the top of the Jacobean Tower after her lover left her. She is said to walk the corridors and rooms at the front of the Hall, particularly the bedrooms.
The second ghost relates to one of the former owners of the Hall, Lord Surtee. One of the Lord's many children was 'ill of mind' and his unique way of coping with this was to chain the child up to one of the Great Hall's Fireplaces... day & night . The laughter and crying of young children is sometimes heard in this area of the Great Hall.
Enjoy your stay!

Beautiful **Elvey Farm** dates back to the early 15th Century. Th small country hotel is situated in Pluckley, the Most Haunted Village in England, and is renowned for its Ghostly Guests... Elvey Farm is a medieval farmstead in the village of Pluckley, Kent. The Hall House was built in 1430 and little has changed since then. Once used as a 75 acre farm for cereals and sheep, Elvey is now run as a small country hotel. Guests stay i the converted stable block and barn, and enjoy brand new contemporary bathrooms and excellent personal service, wi glorious views over the Kent countryside.

Whether you're sipping champagne on the veranda outside your suite, or you're riding your own horse through our excellent bridleways, you'll be surrounded by the quietest, the prettiest and the most idyllic countryside in Kent.

At breakfast you have fresh eggs from our own chickens, sausages from local farms, tomatoes and fried potatoes from our own gardens. In the evenings, you can sample wine or cider from Kent's vineyards, and admire crafts from local artis Elvey has been run by local people for centuries. That's why we say Elvey is Kentish to the core.

Elvey Farm

Elvey Lane , Pluckley
KENT TN27 0SU
Tel: 01233 840 442
Email:
bookings@elveyfarm.co.uk
www.elveyfarm.co.uk

HOTEL FEATURES

- Double rooms in the converted stables
- Brand new contemporary en-suite bathrooms
- Stunning views across the fields.
- A beautiful Dining Room with low beams
- Roaring log fire
- Fabulous Full English Breakfast

Haunted History

hauntedhotelguide
.com

According to the Guinness Book of Records, Pluckley is the most haunted village in England. There have been numerous sightings – and at last count, there are 42 Ghosts in the village alone. **Elvey Farm** has long been known as the only haunted hotel in the area. Edward Brett, a farmer at Elvey, is reputed to have shot himself here. He may have died over a hundred years ago, but many say Edward is still here. The previous owners of the farm saw Mr Brett on many occasions walking the corridors at night. Many guests have seen him too... Some say he is so vivid, it's as though he's alive today. Guests have reported a strange smell, resembling burning hay. There have been reports of a poltergeist – and paranormal investigators have confirmed the farm is bristling with activity. The present owners have already experienced Edward Brett – his voice has twice been heard whispering in the old dairy where he shot himself.

Many people come to Pluckley to find the ghosts – many people descend on Elvey Farm. At Hallowe'en, the whole village is packed. But there's far more than a ghost here. It's an idyllic location, surrounded by fields, orchards and hop gardens. It's Kent at its best – ghosts and all...

Ffolkes Arms at Hillington is a friendly family run hotel which offers first class commodation and a wide range of services and facilities. It holds a dark cret however, as it is reputedly haunted by a young nanny who committed cide...

e hotel, which bears the name of the Ffolkes family, was constructed over ee hundred years ago and became well known as a very popular aching Inn, being located on the main mailing route from the Midlands in Norwich. For a period of time the attic rooms of the hotel were used as an ernight gaol for the prison carriages on their way to the prison in Norwich. s now provides the hotel with 20 bedrooms, all tastefully furnished, and mplete with en-suite facilities. The rooms also ensure added comfort; each ving twin or double beds, remote control colour television, direct dial ephone, tea making facilities, hair dryer and trouser press.

Ffolkes Arms Hotel

Lynn Road, Hillington,
King's Lynn,
Norfolk, PE31 6BJ
www.ffolkes-arms-hotel.co.uk

HOTEL FEATURES
- En suite facilities
- Television
- Direct Dial Telephone
- Tea and Coffee Making Facilities
- Hair Dryer

aunted History hauntedhotelguide.com

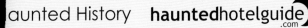

e **Ffolkes Arms** is reputedly haunted by a young nanny, who apparently rew herself out of one of the attic bedrooms during the latter part of the th century and was, quite gruesomely, embedded on the iron railings hich then ran along the front of the inn.
er benign spirit is known to wander the bedrooms and corridors of this eautiful hotel.

he **Schooner Hotel,** situated in Alnmouth, Northumberland has been twice warded the title of The Most Haunted Hotel in Great Britain and is reputed to ave over 60 individual ghosts...
he Famous Schooner Hotel and Restaurant, a Listed 17th century coaching nn only 100 yards from the beach, river and golf course, has been the hub of Alnmouth village since its first customer back in the 1600's, and remains one of he most well known and respected hotels in the North East of England. Notable persons said to have stayed at The Schooner include Charles Dickens, John Wesley, Basil Rathbone, Douglas Bader and even King George II and there is always the chance of meeting our Resident Ghost - "Parson Smyth"! There is little doubting that our motto "Comfort with Character" is ustly deserved, and this can be seen by the number of guests who return to The Famous Schooner time and time again.

Schooner Hotel

Alnmouth, Alnwick
Northumberland NE66 2RS
Tel: +44 (0)1665 830216
Email: info@theschoonerhotel.co.uk
www.theschoonerhotel.co.uk

HOTEL FEATURES
- En suite facilities
- Television
- Tea and coffee making facilities
- Licensed Bar & Restaurant
- Conference Facilities

Haunted History hauntedhotelguide.com

The **Schooner Hotel** has been twice awarded the title of The Most Haunted Hotel in Great Britain by The Poltergeist Society and is reputed to have over 60 individual ghosts. The hotel has a somewhat unclear history, but there are reports of suicides, murders and even of babies being thrown into the fire. It is a very 'active' hotel with over 3000 recent sightings, ranging from ghosts dressed in military uniform to apparitions of a little boy. The sound of screaming, whispers and knocking are also a very common occurrence and are regularly experienced by staff and guests alike.

Stunning **Chillingham Castle** with its alarming dungeons and torture chamb has, since the twelve-hundreds, been continuously owned by the family of the Earls Grey and their relations. The Castle is also home to a number a ghosts, the most famous being the 'Blue Boy'...

In a glorious and secluded setting in Northumberland's famously beautiful countryside, Chillingham Castle offers holidaymakers the unbelievable experience of staying in a medieval fortress.

Parts of the Castle and the coach house have been converted into comfortable holiday apartments, offering the opportunity for a memorable holiday.

The extensive grounds are accessible to holiday makers. Within a few miles the coast and being in close proximity to several golf courses, Chillingham is ideally situated for a unique holiday, with fishing, golf and stately home visits

Chillingham Castle

Chillingham, Alnwick
Northumberland NE66 5NJ
Tel: +44 (0)1668 215359
Email:
enquiries@chillingham-castle.com
www.chillingham-castle.com

HOTEL FEATURES

- Colour television, microwave, fridge and electric cooker
- Stunning Grounds
- Log burning stoves
- Logs and kindling for fires

Haunted History   **haunted**hotelguide.com

We have a number of ghosts at **Chillingham Castle**. The most famous is the "Blue Boy" whose moans are often heard around midnight. These noises hav been traced to a spot near a passage cut through a ten foot wall, behind which the bones of a young boy and fragments of blue clothing were discovered! People sleeping in that room even today, have been known to see the figure of a young boy dressed in blue, and surrounded by light. Another ghost, Lady Mary Berkeley, searches for her husband who ran off wi her sister. Lady Mary, desolate and broken hearted, lived in the castle by herself with only her baby daughter as a companion. The rustle of her dress can be heard as she passes people by...

The **George Hotel** is a fifteenth century coaching inn set in the heart of Oxfordshire. In the days of the stagecoach it provided a welcome haven for many an aristocrat including the first Duchess of Marlborough, Sarah Churchil However, in more recent times we have seen famous guests of a different hue such as author DH Lawrence.

The Buildings of The George Hotel have changed little since their heyday as c coaching inn. It retains all the beauty and charm of those days whilst offering every modern amenity.

The Hotel provides 17 en-suite bedrooms set in peaceful surroundings: all individually decorated and furnished with fine antiques. Our owners have created a décor which suits the requirements of modern times and facilities whilst maintaining the spirit of the past.

The George Hotel

High Street, Dorchester-on-Thames
Oxfordshire OX10 7HH
Tel: 01865 340404
E-mail: info@thegeorgedorch-ester.co.uk
www.thegeorgedorchester.co.uk

HOTEL FEATURES

- En suite bathroom
- Colour TV • Alarm clock Radio
- Direct Dial Telephone
- Cathedral or garden views
- Tea & coffee making facilities

Haunted History   **haunted**hotelguide.com

This beautiful hotel is directly opposite Dorchester Abbey and is well renowned for its spectral visitors. Being so close to the Abbey it is little surprise that a mischievous monk often frequents Room 6. The spirit of an old lady has also been 'picked up' by a number of mediums. She is present in Room 3 of the hotel and on occasion, her reflection has been seen through the windows.

Another visitor to the **George Hotel** frequents one of the bedrooms in particular – The Vicar's Room. This room is reputed to be haunted by a ghost of a sad-looking girl dressed in a white gown.

e beautiful **Bull Hotel** at Long Melford dates back to the Fifteenth Century.
e Ghost of Richard Evered, murdered there in 1648, still roams the Hotel...
riginal timber work, both outside and inside is unusually well preserved.
t of the exterior was discovered in 1935 when a hundred year old brick
nt was removed. On a beam in the lounge is carved a 'Wildman' or
oodwose', a mysterious being frequently depicted in the decoration of the
ddle ages, reputedly to ward off evil spirits.
e Bull Hotel, boasting 25 en-suite bedrooms, was tastefully refurbished in
03 and is renowned for its excellent cuisine and chef's specialities...

aunted History **haunted**hotelguide

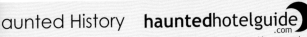

e **Bull Hotel** is quite famous for its ghosts. Indeed it is mentioned in a number
books on the subject. According to the legend, a man named "Richard
vered" was murdered there in 1648. The crime had a strange twist however,
s the victim's body disappeared overnight! It is said that the spirit of Richard
vered roams the Bull Hotel now.
long with a number of apparitions, the Bull is also known for its poltergeist
ctivity: a large oak door opens and closes by itself; chairs move around the
ining room of their own accord and the sound of breaking crockery has
een heard by several guests. One person even had a copper jug thrown at
hem.
's definitely a place we would recommend!

Bull Hotel

Hall Street, Long Melford
Sudbury, Suffolk CO10 9JG
Tel: 01787 378494
Email:
bull.longmelford@greeneking.co.uk
www.thebull-hotel.com

HOTEL FEATURES

- Colour Television
- Mini Stereo
- Direct Dial Telephones
- Ironing Boards • Irons •Hairdryers
- Tea & coffee making facilities

---

teeped in history **Brownsover Hall** is now a fabulous hotel. It is said to be
aunted by One Handed Boughton - a former inhabitant of the hall who lost
is arm during Elizabethan times...
he Hall Hotel is a Grade 11 Listed Victorian Gothic mansion nestling in 7 acres
f woodland and garden. This magnificent building has a dramatic interior
with sweeping staircase and crackling log fires. With rich colours and plenty of
character and charm the Brownsover Hall Hotel has a distinct unique charm.
The Hall borders three counties, making it the ideal base for visiting Warwick,
Stratford-upon-Avon and the North Cotswolds.

Haunted History **haunted**hotelguide

A member of the Boughton-Leigh family, who had his hand severed at the
time of Queen Elizabeth I, is reputed to haunt **Brownsover Hall** despite many
attempts to exorcise the ghost. The spirit was finally imprisoned in a glass
bottle and thrown into a nearby lake. Everything was fine at the Hall until the
bottle was discovered by a group of fishermen and returned to the Hall
around 100 years ago...
The spirit of One-handed Boughton, as he was known, is reputed to haunt the
grounds, and many unexplained noises, footsteps and voices can often be
heard emanating from the tower...

Brownsover Hall

Brownsover Lane, Old Brownsover
Rugby,Warwickshire CV21 1HU
Tel: +44 (0)1788 546100
Email:
gm.brownsoverhall@foliohotels.com
www.foliohotels.com/brownsoverhall

HOTEL FEATURES

- Gilbert Scott Restaurant
- Warwick Bar
- WiFi internet access
- Nearest Rail Link: Rugby 1mile
- Nearest Airport: Birmingham

Built in 1220 and reputed to be the oldest purpose built hotel in England, The **Old Bell Hotel** is still offering quintessentially English warmth, comfort and hospitality nearly eight hundred years later.

Standing alongside Malmesbury's medieval Abbey, in England's first capital, the hotel provides outstanding levels of service and retains the ambience of a bygone age.

There are 31 en suite bedrooms, 15 in the main house, each furnished in an individual style, some with antique furniture, and a further 16 in the Coach House

The Old Bell Hotel

Abbey Row, Malmesbury
Wiltshire SN16 0AG
Tel: 01666 822344
Email:
www.oldbellhotel.com

HOTEL FEATURES

- En Suite Facilities
- Televisions with integral
- DVD players, Sky TV
- Wired broadband internet access.

Haunted History haunted hotelguide.com

The **Old Bell Hotel** is renowned for its mysterious goings on - which is not surprising as the east wing of the hotel is built directly on part of the former abbey.

The hotel's most famous ghost is said to be the spirit of a lady who was unhappily married in the abbey. Her ghost, known as the Grey Lady, has reputedly been seen wandering about the bedrooms, in particular the James Ody Room.

Many more strange happenings have occurred at the Old Bell including glasses rising into the air and smashing by themselves in the Danvers Room; wardrobes mysteriously jamming themselves against doors in the Foe Room and night porters reporting a cold atmosphere when walking down the corridor towards the Salon... Could these experiences all be attributed to the Grey Lady... or are there more mischievous spirits at the Old Bell?

The **Station Hotel**, originally built in the early 20th Century has played host to many famous guests, including Bob Hope and Laurel and Hardy. The spirit of a girl murdered in the hotel is said to roam the corridors...

The Station Hotel offers a warm and friendly atmosphere. Set in the heart of the Midlands, the hotel is easily accessible from Junction 2 of the M5 which is only five minutes drive away.

Originally built in 1910, The Station was demolished in 1936 in order to build a larger hotel. This became particularly popular with theatrical artists playing the Hippodrome Theatre, once situated opposite. Laurel & Hardy, Bob Hope, Bing Crosby and George Formby are amongst the famous names that have stayed at this historic Hotel.

Station Hotel

Castle Hill, Dudley
West Midlands DY1 4RA
Tel: +44 (0)1384 253418
Email:
sales@stationhoteldudley.co.uk
www.stationhoteldudley.co.uk

HOTEL FEATURES

- En suite bathroom
- Colour TV
- Radio
- Tea & Coffee Making Facilities
- Wedding Facilities

Haunted History haunted hotelguide.com

Going back to the beginning, researching the building was almost impossible due to the misplacement of many archive records. However, it is up to you to decide whether the folklore stories told about the hotel over the years are true or not.....

The story tells of a hotel manager who enticed a servant girl into the cellar. Spurning his advances and threatening to tell his wife, the girl was murdered by the hotel manager. He strangled and stabbed her then hid her body in a barrel. 'Most Haunted's Derek Acorah 'picked up' the ghost of the murdered girl as well as the spirit of writer George Lawley and the spirits of two young children. The other, as yet unnamed spirit Acorah picked up on, is rumoured to be sitting waiting for someone in the infamous ROOM 214.

nning **Hazlewood Castle** is steeped in history and was
t mentioned in the Doomsday Book carried out for King
lliam. Ghostly apparitions and sounds are regularly
perienced...

t in seventy-seven acres of tranquil parkland Hazlewood
astle, a former monastery and retreat has been
oughtfully and tastefully designed to offer a distinctly
fferent lifestyle experience. Hazlewood combines the
egance of the Castle with the excellence of the food
nd service offered to all our guests. Whether visiting
azlewood for the first time with friends or as a delegate at
ne of our major conferences you will always be greeted
ith a warm welcome.We have twenty-one bedrooms
nd suites at Hazlewood. Nine of them are situated in the
ain castle and twelve are in our annex area "St
argaret's" which is located in our picturesque Courtyard.
ll bedrooms are beautifully decorated to the highest
andards, with great care taken to enhance their natural
eauty. All bedrooms are individual and vary in shape and
zes, designed to provide a relaxing haven full of
nickknacks (and little rubber ducks!).

Hazlewood Castle

Paradise Lane, Hazlewood
Tadcaster
North Yorkshire LS24 9NJ
Tel: 01937 535353
Email: info@hazlewood-castle.co.uk
www.hazlewood-castle.co.uk

HOTEL FEATURES

- Beautiful Restaurant
- Weddings
- Satellite television
- Tea and Coffee making Facilities
- Modem Links for E-mail
  and Internet Access
- En suite Bathrooms

Haunted History   hauntedhotelguide.com

Hazlewood Castle is steeped in history and it is no surprise that it has its fair share of ghosts.
Many of the bedrooms throughout the hotel are haunted. Tansy bedroom, for example, is mentioned in
a ghost book as having a monk dressed in black 'making his presence felt' in the room.
Staff and guests alike have seen and felt strange presences in Lavender bedroom, Rose Bedroom
and the Jasmine Suite.
Downstairs in the hotel, a priest has been seen walking from the direction of the Great Hall into the
Library and then disappear. As the castle was a former monastery, the monks and priests would walk
from the Great Hall to the Tower to go down into the cloisters, which is where the fireplace is now
positioned in the Library
Voices have also been heard at Hazlewood Castle... A voice saying "goodnight" was heard by a chef
as she was leaving the Restaurant Anise to enter Reception but no-one was there, and over the
Christmas period of 2003 one guest complained repeatedly overnight of a baby crying keeping her
awake. However, no babies were in the adjoining rooms.

Mosborough Hall

High Street, Mosborough
Sheffield
South Yorkshire S20 5EA
Tel: 0114 248 4353
Email: hotel@mosboroughhall.co.uk
www.mosboroughhall.co.uk

Beautiful **Mosborough Hall** dates back hundreds of years and is steeped in history. It is now a luxurious hotel and is also home to a number of ghosts, including the White Lady and a Spectral Dog...

A wealth of quality, service and history wait for you at Mosborough Hall Hotel. The Hotel was lovingly restored in 1974 from a magnificent 750 year old Manor House. No expense has been spared, with each room having been carefully restored and decorated to retain the historic ambience that is rarely enjoyed today. An ancient doorway leads from the friendly reception to the oak bar, with minstrel gallery and old stone mullioned windows, inviting you to relax in comfort as you take a drink, perhaps before enjoying the superb cuisine for which the restaurant has been long celebrated. The Restaurant consistently maintains its Rosettes award-winning standard with fresh home made breads, chocolates and patisseries.

Mosborough Hall has a selection of 47 rooms to cover all tastes; from Four Poster Feature Rooms with authentic wall panelling for that special occasion, to recently renovated Contemporary Rooms.

HOTEL FEATURES

- Beautiful Award-winning Restaurant
- Weddings
- Conference Facilities
- Satellite Television
- Tea and Coffee making Facilities
- Telephone Modem Links
  for E-mail and Internet Access

Haunted History

haunted hotelguide
.com

Mosborough Hall was an ancient Manor House, the earliest parts of which date back to medieval times. It survives today as Mosborough Hall Hotel and still retains its stately charm behind a somewhat foreboding exterior appearance. Partly hidden by tall, stark trees, an air of mystery is enhanced by a high stone wall which hides the intimacies of the Hall from passers-by using the quiet Hallow Lane. There was a doorway through the wall, which was used by servants when they collected milk or eggs from the farm opposite. Many tales were told of strange noises and voices heard around this doorway, sufficient enough to raise a prickle on the back of the neck when walking past in the dim light of a fading evening.

Stories of a doctor waking up in his bed dripping with blood, a spectral dog and The White Lady of Mosborough Hall are enough to make the blood run cold. The White Lady, thought to have been a governess at the hotel killed by the squire with whom she was in love, is regularly seen throughout the hotel.

utiful **Comlongon Castle** dates back to the 1300s.
truly breathtaking building is now a luxurious hotel.
hotel also boasts a ghost - that of the 'Green
dy', thought to be the spirit of Marion Carruthers...

mlongon Castle, near Gretna in Scotland, is a
tored 14th Century Medieval Scottish Castle
dding Venue and luxurious Baronial Hotel with 14
ividually themed luxury en-suite 4-poster bedrooms.
e wedding castle hotel has two Oak panelled
taurants for receptions and a private residents' bar.
r chefs specialise in local produce, changing their
nus daily.
s Romantic Medieval Castle is the perfect wedding
nue for your wedding castle reception or
lebration in Scotland. Steeped in Scottish Border
tory, Comlongon Castle is more than just fantastic
tel – it has fantastic displays of armour, weapons and
nners, whilst the opulent bedrooms boast 4-poster
ds and jacuzzis providing a stunning blend of
edieval and modern luxury.

Comlongon Castle

Clarencefield , Dumfries
Dumfries and Galloway DG1 4NA
Tel: 01387 870283
Email:
reception@comlongon.co.uk
www.comlongon.com

HOTEL FEATURES

- Four-Poster Suites
- En suite Facilities
- Breathtaking Surroundings
- Jacuzzi Baths

Haunted History

hauntedhotelguide⬤

Marion Carruthers is a presence that has been felt within **Comlongon Castle** for over four centuries. Since her death in 1570 there have been numerous sightings of a "Green Lady" wandering the grounds of the estate. The smell of apples often precedes these apparitions.

Over the last decade sightings have been concentrated upon one room in particular. Guests have reported numerous sightings of a figure in a long dress either sitting on the four-poster bed or drifting between the bed and door. Most stories from guests mention the moving of jewellery, particularly watches and bracelets, from one location to another.

Sightings at one period numbered almost once a month, so much so that staff began to talk of the suite as "Marion's room". Upon the introduction of new jacuzzis in several rooms, including Marion's, it seemed the obvious choice to name this as the Carruthers suite.

If you wish to book this room please inform reception. We are always interested in information you gather...

Ardoe House Hotel

South Deeside Road, Blairs
Aberdeen AB12 5YP
Tel: 01224 860 600
Email: H6626@accor.com
www.mercure.com

HOTEL FEATURES

- 24 hour room service
- Satellite Television
- Tea and Coffee making Facilities
- Swimming Pool
- State of the Art Beauty Salon

Ardoe House dates back to 1878. The hotel's traditional decor including wood panelled walls, enormous fireplaces and a grand staircase are not th only reminders of its past - some of the hotel's previous inhabitants still remc Ardoe House is a luxurious modern hotel, beautifully crafted from an imposi 19th century mansion house and inspired by the royal residence of Balmorc Castle, a few miles upstream.

Throwing open your window to capture the morning light as it spills over the River Dee is one of the pure delights of a stay at the Ardoe House. We've created over one hundred bedrooms in this historic setting, each one capturing the distinctly romantic mood of the surrounding countryside. Depending on your mood you can choose to dine in our elegant AA rosett winning restaurant or enjoy a meal in the relaxed surroundings of the Laird's Bar, where you can enjoy a dram in front of a crackling fire in Winter. It is, quite simply, beautiful.

Haunted History   haunted hotelguide.com

Ardoe House is no stranger to mysterious noises and ghostly apparitions. The hotel is said to be haunted by the white lady, thought to be Katherine Ogston, the wife of soap merchant Alexander Milne Ogston. Her spirit has been seen throughout the hotel but most of the 'activity' seems to centre round a portrait of Katherine on the main stairs.

There are conflicting reports as to who this ghost is. Whilst some maintain tha the White Lady is the spirit of Katherine Ogston, others believe that the ghost the spirit of the daughter of a former owner who committed suicide...

Maesmawr Hall Hotel

Caersws, Powys, SY17 5SF.
Tel: 01686 688255
Fax: 01686 688410
Email:
information@maesmawr.co.uk
www.maesmawr.co.uk

HOTEL FEATURES

- En suite rooms
- Stunning Views
- Welsh Coastline and attractions nearby

Maesmawr Hall Hotel, Caersws is situated in the beautiful valley of the Severn This stunning period house is privately owned and personally supervised by the resident proprietors, Tim and Matthew Lewis.

The hotel is one of the most complete and picturesque of the old half-timbered houses of Montgomeryshire and a fine example of the central chimney timber-framed houses which are characteristic of Mid Wales. The general appearance of the house suggests a mid 17th Century dwelling but it has been established that the house was in existence before 1600. The hotel has 17 en-suite bedrooms with modern facilities, many of which have been recently refurbished to a high standard and offer stunning views over the grounds and the breathtaking countryside beyond

Whether it's simply an overnight stay with bed and breakfast, or a longer holiday, Maesmawr Hall combines the quiet tranquillity of a country house with the atmosphere of a popular venue.

Haunted History   haunted hotelguide.com

All old houses with the slightest self respect claim to possess a ghost and **Maesmawr Hall** is no exception! The Grey Lady, an unknown spectre and Robin Drwg (Wicked Robin), assuming the form of a bull, are said to roam the Hall.

Robin Drwg was a renowned rapscallion in his day and it appears that he caused much mischief and alarm to those who encountered him. He was eventually overcome by the efforts of seven parsons of undoubted ability and laid in Llyn Tarw (the Bull's Pool)....

Whether the endeavours of the worthy gentlemen were successful or not is a matter of conjecture, but it is claimed that his half man/half beastly form still lurks!

ig-y-Nos Castle nestles in the lovely Upper Swansea ley next to the River Tawe. The castle was the former me of opera diva, Adelina Patti and is now a autiful hotel with a very haunted history...

ig-y-nos Castle is situated in an area of outstanding tural beauty. With its wonderful location and the thentic ambience of a Welsh Castle, Craig-y-Nos s plenty to offer. Whether you want a relaxing break, over night stay, or if you are joining us as part of a ction, you can be sure of a totally unique perience.

e Castle benefits from a number of bars and taurants and is fully equipped to cater for nferences and wedding parties.

ig-y-nos Castle has a wide variety of commodation ranging from budget rooms to en- ite and luxury guest rooms overlooking the gardens. ch room is unique in design and is furnished in a ditional fashion in keeping with the Castle's history. e castle also benefits from Spa facilities, gymnasium d spa that enjoy unsurpassed panoramic views of e Brecon Beacons.

Craig-y-Nos Castle

Powys SA9 1GL
Email:
bookings_craigynos@hotmail.com
www.craigynoscastle.com

HOTEL FEATURES

- Fantastic Location
- Character Bedrooms
- Ghost Tours
- Beacons Spa Facilities
- Wonderful Public Rooms
- En suite Facilities

Haunted History

hauntedhotelguide**.com**

Old castles, with their colourful and often turbulent histories, often conjure up pictures of ghosts and paranormal goings-on. **Craig-y-Nos Castle** is no exception and has established a reputation amongst "ghost watchers" who have experienced apparitions, poltergeist activity and strange noises first hand. As the former home of Opera Diva Adelina Patti, who was embalmed in its cellars, and later as a Tuberculosis Hospital, where many succumbed to their illness, the Castle has a rich history of both dramatic and tragic events...

As well as being haunted by the Opera Diva herself, the Castle is home to many more spirits including a small boy accompanied by a soldier, often seen at the bottom of the staircase. The Nicolini Bar, formerly the Library of Patti's second husband Ernesto Nicolini, is haunted by a male spirit who is often heard shouting orders. There is also a well documented malevolent spirit who resides in the cellar.

A number of television programmes have been produced illustrating the paranormal activities at Craig-y-Nos Castle and due to the overwhelming interest from the general public wanting to experience them for themselves the castle now organises "Ghost Watch Tours".

Stunning **Kinnitty Castle** has everything you would expect from an historic castle hotel and much more. We have our own resident ghost – The Monk!

Kinnitty Castle is located in the heart of Ireland, close to the picturesque village of Kinnitty in County Offaly. Approximately one hour 30 minutes from both Dublin and Shannon airports, it nestles in the foothills of the beautiful Slieve Bloom Mountains and is in Ireland's o designated Environment Park.

The whole area is steeped in Irish history and there is a wide range of things to see and do.

The hotel has 37 en suite bedrooms, all decorated in keeping with the castle's romantic old-world style. Wi two restaurants offering a selection of delicious dishe: and two bars, the hotel is the ideal venue for holidays and special occasions alike. Our private panelled banqueting hall provides a secluded setting for weddings, conferences and themed functions. Excellent cuisine, fine wines, open turf fires, candleligh and excellent service create a very warm and welcoming atmosphere that is special to Kinnitty Castle.

Kinnitty Castle

Kinnitty, Birr
County Offaly
Ireland
Tel: +353 (0)509 37318
Email: info@kinnittycastle.com
www.kinnittycastle.com

HOTEL FEATURES

- Luxury en suite accommodation
- Bars and Restaurants
- Gate Lodge Spa
- Activities such as shooting, fishing, tennis & equestrian sports

Haunted History

hauntedhotelguide
.com

The Castle has a long and colourful history which dates back to ancient times. Located on an ancient druidic ceremonial ground, where leylines cross and mystical forces are prevalent, the area around Kinnitty is considered by many to be a very mystical and magical place. The castle is also known for its infamous ghostly guest... the monk.

The monk has often been seen wandering through the glorious Banqueting Hall, stunning both staff and visitors alike. He has been known to communicate with staff members on occasion, sometimes even prophesying about future events which have unbelievably come true! Other rooms throughout the castle are haunted, in particular the Geraldine Room and the Elizabeth room where eerie presences have been felt.

Skirrid Mountain Inn is situated in Llanvihangel Crucorney; a small village off the A465; approximately 5 miles north from the centre of Abergavenny d 18 miles from Hereford.

reputed to be the oldest Inn in Wales and it's history can be traced back ar as the Norman Conquest.

inn has an ancient wood-panelled restaurant where you can sit and by delicious home cooked food from the menu. There are fireplaces with l fires, two bars, one with a pool table, an old ship's bell for calling last ers, and three comfortable luxury visitor's bedrooms, two with four poster ds.

The Skirrid Inn
Llanvihangel Crucorney,
Abergavenny,
Monmouthshire, NP7 8DH
Tel: 01873 890258
www.skirridmountaininn.co.uk/

HOTEL FEATURES
- En suite facilities
- Four-poster beds
- Colour Television
- Tea and Coffee making
- Wonderful views

aunted History **haunted**hotelguide.com

e **Skirrid Inn,** the oldest in Wales, is well known for its haunting happenings d there's good reason to take these "sightings" seriously due to the inn's uesome history. The Skirrid has been an inn since 1110 but is most famous for use as Judge Jeffrey's courtroom in the wake of the Monmouth rebellion. e brutal judge famously hanged 180 rebels in 1685 from a beam beneath e Skirrid's staircase. The beam stands today and bears chaffing marks from e hangman's rope.

o-one can be entirely sure who actually haunts the bedrooms and stairways the Inn but many people believe that 'hanging' Judge Jeffreys could not st, or that some of the 180 people he sent to the gallows have come back r revenge.

unning **Ross Castle**, situated on the shores of Lough Sheelin, dates back to 536 and, not surprisingly, is steeped in history. The ghosts of two star-crossed vers are often witnessed...

uated amidst majestic trees in the tranquil countryside on the County eath and Cavan border, Ross Castle commands magnificent views of ough Sheelin, a 4500 acre lake famous for its brown trout and liberally ocked perch and large pike.

e secluded setting and spacious, comfortable accommodation offer the sitor an exclusive retreat. The Castle is the perfect place to relax and nwind, away from the stresses and strains of modern city life, or as a venue r a private party or function.

Ross Castle
Mountnugent
County Meath
Ireland
Tel: +353 (0) 43 81286
Email : book@ross-castle.com
www.ross-castle.com

HOTEL FEATURES
- Tea and Coffee making facilities.
- En suite Bedrooms
- Four-Poster Room
- Use of Leisure Facilities at Ross House

Haunted History **haunted**hotelguide.com

all started back in 1536, when **Ross Castle** was first built. Legend has it that e Lord of Delvin, who built the castle, had a beautiful daughter, Sabina, ho happened to fall in love with Orwin, the son of an Irish Lord. Fearing that heir love would not be accepted by their families, they decided to elope. hey set off in a sail boat but were unfortunately caught in a terrible storm. rwin was tipped overboard and was killed instantly. Sabina was thrown out f the boat and was rescued by onlookers. They brought her back to the astle where she slept for three days. When she finally awoke, she found rwin, who was laid out in the chapel on the grounds of Ross Castle. She died hortly after that.

England and Wales • Counties

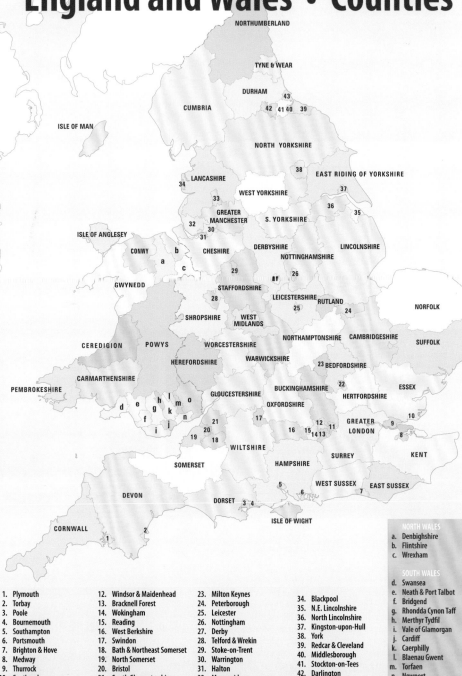

NORTHUMBERLAND

TYNE & WEAR

DURHAM
43

CUMBRIA
42 41 40 39

ISLE OF MAN

NORTH YORKSHIRE

38

LANCASHIRE
34
EAST RIDING OF YORKSHIRE
37

WEST YORKSHIRE
33
36
35

GREATER
MANCHESTER
32
30
S. YORKSHIRE
31

ISLE OF ANGLESEY

CONWY
b
CHESHIRE
DERBYSHIRE
LINCOLNSHIRE
a
NOTTINGHAMSHIRE
c
29
26

GWYNEDD
STAFFORDSHIRE
28
LEICESTERSHIRE
RUTLAND
25
24
NORFOLK

SHROPSHIRE
WEST
MIDLANDS

CEREDIGION
POWYS
WORCESTERSHIRE
NORTHAMPTONSHIRE
CAMBRIDGESHIRE
SUFFOLK
HEREFORDSHIRE
WARWICKSHIRE
23 BEDFORDSHIRE

CARMARTHENSHIRE
22
ESSEX

PEMBROKESHIRE
GLOUCESTERSHIRE
BUCKINGHAMSHIRE
HERTFORDSHIRE
d e g h l m o
OXFORDSHIRE
10
f k n
17
GREATER
9
i j
21
16 15 11
LONDON
20
14 13
8
19
18
12

WILTSHIRE
SURREY
KENT

SOMERSET
HAMPSHIRE
WEST SUSSEX
EAST SUSSEX
5
6
7

DEVON
DORSET
3 4

ISLE OF WIGHT

CORNWALL
2
1

1. Plymouth	12. Windsor & Maidenhead	23. Milton Keynes	34. Blackpool
2. Torbay	13. Bracknell Forest	24. Peterborough	35. N.E. Lincolnshire
3. Poole	14. Wokingham	25. Leicester	36. North Lincolnshire
4. Bournemouth	15. Reading	26. Nottingham	37. Kingston-upon-Hull
5. Southampton	16. West Berkshire	27. Derby	38. York
6. Portsmouth	17. Swindon	28. Telford & Wrekin	39. Redcar & Cleveland
7. Brighton & Hove	18. Bath & Northeast Somerset	29. Stoke-on-Trent	40. Middlesborough
8. Medway	19. North Somerset	30. Warrington	41. Stockton-on-Tees
9. Thurrock	20. Bristol	31. Halton	42. Darlington
10. Southend	21. South Gloucestershire	32. Merseyside	43. Hartlepool
11. Slough	22. Luton	33. Blackburn with Darwen	

NORTH WALES
a. Denbighshire
b. Flintshire
c. Wrexham

SOUTH WALES
d. Swansea
e. Neath & Port Talbot
f. Bridgend
g. Rhondda Cynon Taff
h. Merthyr Tydfil
i. Vale of Glamorgan
j. Cardiff
k. Caerphilly
l. Blaenau Gwent
m. Torfaen
n. Newport
o. Monmouthshire

symbols

	Totally non-smoking		Pets Welcome
	Children Welcome		Christmas Breaks
	Suitable for Disabled Guests		Licensed

Padstow, Cornwall

WHATEVER SORT of holiday destination you're looking for, you'll find it in South-West England. As well as the elegant shops and Georgian crescents of Bath, other south-west towns have the very latest in big shopping centres, speciality shops and nightlife. There are stretches of wild moorland, chalk hills, limestone gorges and thatched-house villages and there are miles of golden sand washed by Atlantic breakers. From Orcombe Rocks, Exmouth to Studland Bay in Dorset, the Jurassic Coast Natural World Heritage Site gives a unique insight into life in the past through the rocks exposed along the 95 miles of beautiful coastline.

Devon has both coast and countryside. Plymouth on the south coast has been a naval base of the greatest importance to the defence of the realm since the days of Sir Francis Drake. The city was hastily rebuilt after destruction in the Second World War, but nothing can spoil the glorious vista of the Sound viewed from Plymouth Hoe where Drake finished his game of bowls.

Cornwall reaches into the Atlantic Ocean for almost 100 miles. Take a walk along any part of this strikingly beautiful coast, enjoy a cream tea in one of the charming villages sheltering in a cove and you will understand why Cornwall has been the inspiration for so many artists, novelists and poets. Often free from frost in winter, the soft spring climate favours Cornwall as an ideal destination for holiday breaks.

Say Somerset and most people would automatically think of cider, Cheddar cheese and county cricket matches. But there's a lot more to Somerset – there's Exmoor which is Lorna Doone territory and home to the wild Exmoor ponies and herds of red deer. The National Park of Exmoor has a coastline with some marvellous clifftop walks. Further along this coast are Somerset's main seaside resorts, Minehead and Burnham-on-Sea.

www.westcountrynow.com

South West England
Great Days Out: Visits and Attractions

Flambards
Helston, Cornwall • 01326 573404
www.flambards.co.uk
More than just a theme park, with thrill rides, Flambards Victorian Village, Britain in the Blitz, aviation display, award-winning gardens; restaurants and cafes.

The Eden Project
Near St Austell, Cornwall • 01726 811911
www.edenproject.com
A gateway into the fascinating interaction of plants and people. Two gigantic geodesic conservatories - the Humid Tropics Biome and the Warm Temperate Biome - set amidst landscaped outdoor terraces.

Escot Historic Gardens, Maze and Fantasy Woodlands
Ottery St Mary, Devon • 01404 822188
www.escot-devon.co.uk
For people who love Nature - paths, trails, vistas, beautiful flowers, shrubs and specimen trees. Play areas, pets' corner, restaurant - and lots more!

Diggerland
Cullompton, Devon • 08700 344437
www.diggerland.com
Children as young as 5 can drive the JCBs themselves, toddlers can go on with the help of an adult and adults can use the rides by themselves. Over 15 rides and attractions to test your driving skills, and your hand eye co-ordination.

Abbotsbury Swannery
Near Weymouth, Dorset • 01305 871858
www.abbotsbury-tourism.co.uk
Up to 1000 free-flying swans – help feed them twice daily. Baby swans hatch May/June. AV show,

The Jurassic Coast
East Devon + Dorset
www.jurassiccoast.com
England's first natural World Heritage Site - 95 miles of unspoilt cliffs and beaches, tracing over 185 million years of Earth's history.

Painswick Rococo Garden
Painswick, Gloucs • 01452 813204
www.rococogarden.org.uk
A fascinating step back to a flamboyant and sensual period of English garden design. This gem of a garden, which was originally laid out in the early 18th century, is set in a hidden Cotswold valley with magnificent views of the surrounding countryside.

Haynes Motor Museum
Near Yeovil, Somerset • 01963 440804
www.haynesmotormuseum.co.uk
Magnificent collection of over 250 vintage, veteran and classic cars, and 50 motorcycles.

Jane Austen Centre
Bath • 01225 443000
www.janeausten.co.uk
Explore the Bath of one of the historic city's most famous residents, and its place in her work. Exhibition of Regency clothes, shop with selection of related books, stationery and crafts.

Dunster Water Mill
Dunster, Somerset • 01643 821759
www.dunsterwatermill.co.uk
The West Country's finest working water mill, set alongside the River Avill. See how flour is produced, then visit the Mill Shop where stoneground floor, home-made muesli and other products are available.

Wookey Hole Caves
Near Wells, Somerset • 01749 672243
www.wookey.co.uk
Britain's most spectacular underground caverns, with new attractions and great new facilities. Try making your own paper using original Victorian machinery.

Cholderton Rare Breeds Farm Park
Near Salisbury, Wiltshire • 01980 629438
www.choldertoncharliesfarm.com
Rare and endangered breeds of British farm animals, plus Rabbit World with over 50 varieties. Pig racing (Pork Stakes) in peak season.

Looking for Holiday Accommodation?

for details of hundreds of properties throughout the UK, visit our website
www.holidayguides.com

Cornwall

Please note

All the information in this book is given in good faith in the belief that it is correct. However, the publishers cannot guarantee the facts given in these pages, neither are they responsible for changes in policy, ownership or terms that may take place after the date of going to press. Readers should always satisfy themselves that the facilities they require are available and that the terms, if quoted, still apply.

symbols

Totally non-smoking	Pets Welcome
Children Welcome	Christmas Breaks
Suitable for Disabled Guests	Licensed

Mawgan Porth, Mevagissey, Mousehole

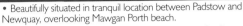

Blue Bay HOTEL, RESTAURANT & LODGES

Trenance, Mawgan Porth, Cornwall TR8 4DA
e-mail: hotel@bluebaycornwall.co.uk
www.bluebaycornwall.co.uk • Tel: 01637 860324

- Beautifully situated in tranquil location between Padstow and Newquay, overlooking Mawgan Porth beach.
- Hotel has two garden suites, one family suite, one family room and five double rooms, all en suite. Twin and single rooms available.
- Dogs welcome; Mawgan Porth beach is dog-friendly.
- 4 individually designed Cornish lodges, all fully equipped (sleep 4-8). All have own balcony or patio area. Linen, towels, electricity incl. Laundry room. Dogs welcome.

Hotel prices from £33pppn • Lodge prices from £50 per Lodge per night.

Kilbol Country House Hotel & Cottages
'Perfect Peace in Hidden Cornwall'

Polmassick, Mevagissey PL26 6HA

A small, cottage-style country hotel set in 5-acre grounds.
Dating back to the 16th century, it has been fully refurbished and offers
8 rooms, as well as two self-catering cottages. Two miles from the Lost
Gardens of Heligan and Mevagissey, and close to the Eden Project. Outdoor swimming pool, riverside walk,
wooded area. No children under 12 years in the hotel. Pets welcome. **Winter & Christmas Breaks available.**

Tel: 01726 842481 • e-mail: Hotel@kilbol-hotel.co.uk • www.kilbol-hotel.co.uk

Lancallan is a large 17th century farmhouse on a working
700-acre dairy and beef farm in a beautiful rural setting, one mile
from Mevagissey. We are close to Heligan Gardens, lovely coastal
walks and sandy beaches, and are well situated for day trips
throughout Cornwall. Also six to eight miles from the Eden
Project (20 minutes' drive). Enjoy a traditional farmhouse
breakfast in a warm and friendly atmosphere.
Accommodation comprises one twin room and two double
en suite rooms (all with colour TV and tea/coffee facilities);
bathroom, lounge and diningroom.
Terms and brochure available on request. SAE please.

Mrs Dawn Rundle, Lancallan Farm, Mevagissey, St Austell PL26 6EW
Tel & Fax: 01726 842284
e-mail: dawn@lancallan.fsnet.co.uk • www.lancallanfarm.co.uk

POLVELLAN FLATS
Mousehole

In Mousehole, a quaint and unspoilt
fishing village, is a personally supervised
and fully equipped self-catering flat, with
full sea views. It has a microwave, cooker,
fridge, and TV; all bedding and towels
provided. Pets welcome. Open all year.

Contact Mr A.G. Wright, 164 Portland Road, Selston, Nottingham NG16 6AN
Tel & Fax: 01773 775347 • e-mail: alang23@hotmail.com

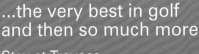

Near Perranporth

Welcome to Greenmeadow Holiday Cottages

Greenmeadow Holiday Cottages are a group of six cottages, situated in a rural setting, yet only 400 yards from the local shop and 500 yards to the pub which serves excellent food and real ale.

The holiday cottages are three miles from Perranporth's golden sands on the north coast of Cornwall.

All sleep up to six people, two cottages welcome pets and all are non-smoking. Three cottages have one en suite bedroom on the ground floor.

•**New for 2007**
Children's Adventure Play Area.

•**There is also a shared BBQ area**

We are open all year and offer short break holiday cottage accommodation out of season.

Greenmeadow Cottages, Bridge Road, Goonhavern, Truro, Cornwall TR4 9NN • 01872 540 483
e-mail: info@greenmeadow-cottages.co.uk
www.greenmeadow-cottages.co.uk

www. polzeath camping .co.uk

North Cornwall camping at its best

Two Great Campsites in One Great Location

Tristram
caravan & campsite

for photos and information on the campsites visit www.polzeathcamping.co.uk

Tristram is one of the closest campsites to the beach in the whole of Cornwall. It caters for both camping and caravans and has stunning views of Polzeath and has brilliant modern facilities.

**For more details call:
01208 862215
or email:
info@tristramcampsite.co.uk**

South Winds
caravan & campsite

Many families love Southwinds because it is so quiet and peaceful. It has beautiful panoramic sea and rural views and is only half a mile from the beach.

**for more details call: 01208 863267
or email: info@southwindscamping.co.uk
or visit our web site at: www.polzeathcamping.co.uk**

MEMBER 2009
Visit Cornwall southwesttourism

Small and welcoming, Hellesveor is an approved farm site situated just one mile from the sweeping beaches and town centre of St Ives. Located on the Land's End road and only five minutes from the bus route for touring the dramatic landscape of West Cornwall and taking spectacular countryside walks.

Hellesveor Caravan and Camping Site
Hellesveor Farm, St Ives TR26 3AD

Laundry facilities on site. Special terms for early and late season.
Campers and touring caravans welcome. Static Caravans for hire. Electrical hook-ups.
Dogs allowed under strict control.
Shop, pub, restaurant, indoor heated pool, tennis courts, fishing, horse riding, pony trekking, golf course, bowling greens and leisure centre all nearby.
SAE for further details.
• SHORT BREAKS - TELEPHONE FOR AVAILABILITY •

Contact G & H Rogers Tel: 01736 795738
www.caravancampingsites.co.uk/cornwall/hellesveor

Other specialised holiday guides from **FHG**

PUBS & INNS OF BRITAIN

COUNTRY HOTELS OF BRITAIN

WEEKEND & SHORT BREAKS IN BRITAIN & IRELAND

THE GOLF GUIDE WHERE TO PLAY, WHERE TO STAY

500 GREAT PLACES TO STAY

SELF-CATERING HOLIDAYS IN BRITAIN

BED & BREAKFAST STOPS IN BRITAIN

CARAVAN & CAMPING HOLIDAYS IN BRITAIN

FAMILY BREAKS IN BRITAIN

Published annually: available in all good bookshops or direct from the publisher:

FHG Guides, Abbey Mill Business Centre, Seedhill, Paisley PA1 1TJ

Tel: 0141 887 0428 • Fax: 0141 889 7204

e-mail: admin@fhguides.co.uk • www.holidayguides.com

Devon

symbols

 Totally non-smoking

 Children Welcome

 Suitable for Disabled Guests

 Pets Welcome

 Christmas Breaks

 Licensed

Fairwater Head Hotel
3 Star Accommodation at Sensible Prices

74%  ★★★

Located in the Devon/Dorset countryside, but close to
Lyme Regis, this beautiful Edwardian Country House Hotel
has all you need for a peaceful and relaxing break.

Dogs Most Welcome and Free of Charge
Countryside location with panoramic views • *AA One Rosette Restaurant*

**The Fairwater Head Hotel
Hawkchurch, Near Axminster, Devon EX13 5TX
Tel: 01297 678349 • Fax: 01297 678459
e-mail: stay@fairwaterheadhotel.co.uk
www.fairwaterheadhotel.co.uk**

Station Lodge, Doddiscombsleigh, Exeter, Devon

Comfortably furnished apartment In the beautiful Teign River valley. Excellent location for exploring Devon's moors, coasts and villages. Kitchen, lounge/diner, en suite bedroom with double bed. Private garden, extensive grounds. Pubs, shops and walks nearby, golf, fishing, horseriding, tennis and swimming pools within 10 miles. Central heating. Colour TV. All linen provided. Parking. Non-smokers only. Well behaved dogs welcome. From £200 per week.

Short Breaks welcome Oct - May. For further details contact:

Ian West, Station House, Doddiscombsleigh, Exeter EX6 7PW • Tel & Fax: 01647 253104
e-mail: enquiries@station-lodge.co.uk • www.station-lodge.co.uk

THE ROYAL OAK INN

Dunsford, Near Exeter EX6 7DA
Tel: 01647 252256

Enjoy a friendly welcome in our traditional Country Pub in the picturesque thatched village of Dunsford. Quiet en suite bedrooms are available in the tastefully converted cob barn. Ideal base for touring Dartmoor, Exeter and the coast, and the beautiful Teign Valley. Real Ale and home-made meals are served.

Well-behaved children and dogs are welcome

Regular dog Kizzy • Resident dog Connie   *Please ring Mark or Judy Harrison for further details.*

Culm Vale Guest House, Stoke Canon, Exeter EX5 4EG

A fine old country house of great charm and character, giving the best of both worlds as we are only three miles to the north of the Cathedral city of Exeter, with its antique shops, yet situated in the heart of Devon's beautiful countryside on the edge of the pretty village of Stoke Canon. An ideal touring centre. Our spacious comfortable Bed and Breakfast accommodation includes full English breakfast, colour TV, tea/coffee facilities, washbasin and razor point in both rooms. Full central heating. Ample free parking. Bed and Breakfast £20 to £27.50 pppn according to room and season. Credit cards accepted.

Telephone & Fax: 01392 841615
e-mail: culmvale@hotmail.com
www.SmoothHound.co.uk/hotels/culm-vale.html

symbols

	Totally non-smoking		Pets Welcome
	Children Welcome		Christmas Breaks
	Suitable for Disabled Guests		Licensed

White Hart
Hotel • Exeter

One of Exeter's most historic inns, the White Hart Hotel retains much of its heritage and charm and yet offers the business or leisure visitor all the facilities and amenities of modern living.

The White Hart boasts 55 en suite rooms. Located in a central position within the old city walls, it's ideally situated to enjoy all the city has to offer, from its famous Gothic Cathedral to the newly opened shopping centre.

The White Hart offers meeting and function rooms with a choice of eating areas, a walled secret garden, an extensive selection of freshly cooked meals, fine cask ales and a comprehensive wine list – all tastes are catered for.

White Hart Hotel
66 South Street, Exeter EX1 1EE
Tel: 01392 279897 • Fax: 01392 250159
E-mail: whitehart.exeter@marstons.co.uk

Blue Ball Inn
formerly The Exmoor Sandpiper Inn

is a romantic Coaching Inn dating in part back to the 13th century, with low ceilings, blackened beams, stone fireplaces and a timeless atmosphere of unspoilt old world charm. Offering visitors great food and drink, a warm welcome and a high standard of accommodation.

The inn is set in an imposing position on a hilltop on Exmoor in North Devon, a few hundred yards from the sea, and high above the twin villages of Lynmouth and Lynton, in an area of oustanding beauty.
The spectacular scenery and endless views attract visitors and hikers from all over the world.

We have 16 en suite bedrooms, comfortable sofas in the bar and lounge areas, and five fireplaces, including a 13th century inglenook. Our extensive menus include local produce wherever possible, such as locally reared meat, amd locally caught game and fish, like Lynmouth Bay lobster; specials are featured daily. We also have a great choice of good wines, available by the bottle or the glass, and a selection of locally brewed beers, some produced specially for us.

Stay with us to relax, or to follow one of the seven circular walks through stunning countryside that start from the Inn. Horse riding for experienced riders or complete novices can be arranged. Plenty of parking. Dogs (no charge), children and walkers are very welcome!

Blue Ball Inn formerly The Exmoor Sandpiper Inn
Countisbury, Lynmouth, Devon EX35 6NE
01598 741263
www.BlueBallinn.com • www.exmoorsandpiper.com

Dating back to the 14th Century, the Rising Sun Hotel is an historic smugglers' Inn nestled in the picturesque harbour of Lynmouth. Over the years it has been gently transformed into an elegant harbourside hotel, whilst retaining its character and charm, with oak panelled dining room and bar, crooked corridors and delightful rooms.

Boasting superior service, comfortable surroundings and fine cuisine combined with truly magnificent views of the harbour and Exmoor coastline, the Rising Sun offers warmth, friendliness and a personal touch whilst providing the highest standards.

All our individually furnished bedrooms are comfortably appointed and possess a charm and individuality seldom found in modern hotels. Most have views over the harbour, assuring guests of an unforgettable experience.

Our restaurant provides an intimate and relaxed ambience. Incorporating the season's produce, maintaining quality and freshness, your meal will reach the highest standards of presentation, taste and creativity.

Rising Sun Hotel & Restaurant
Harbourside, Lynmouth
Devon EX35 6EG
Tel: 01598 753223
Fax: 01598 753480
e-mail: reception@risingsunlynmouth.co.uk
www.specialplace.co.uk

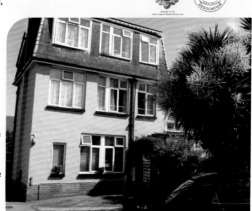

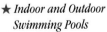

Visit the FHG website
www.holidayguides.com
for details of the wide choice of accommodation
featured in the full range of FHG titles

fun
filled holidays

SHORT BREAKS FROM ONLY £60 family of 4

7 NIGHTS FROM ONLY £100 family of 4

four award winning Holiday Parks set in Devon's breathtaking countryside next to Woolacombe's 3 miles of golden Blue Flag sandy beach!

SEAVIEW Holiday Homes & Luxury Lodges plus great Camping & Touring

over 40 FREE activities...

- 10 Heated Indoor & Outdoor Pools
- Waterslides • Health Suite • Cinema
- Nightly Entertainment & Star Cabaret
- Tennis • Snooker • Crazy Golf • Kid's Clubs
- Kid's Indoor & Outdoor Play Areas • Playzone
- Coarse Fishing Ponds ... Plus so much more!

...and for just a little more

- 10 Pin Bowling
- 17th Century Inn
- Waves Ceramic Studio
- Affiliated Golf Club
- Indoor Bowls Rinks
- Amusement Arcades
- Restaurants & Bars
- Activities Programme

- Kiddy Karts
- Sports Bar
- WaterWalkerz
- Beauty Salon
- Pirate Ship
- Bungee Run
- Climbing Wall
- Swimming Lessons

REGISTER ONLINE FOR LATEST OFFERS!!
woolacombe.com/fsb
01271 870 343

WOOLACOMBE BAY

Dorset

Blandford

FHG Guides

publish a large range of well-known accommodation guides. We will be happy to send you details or you can use the order form at the back of this book.

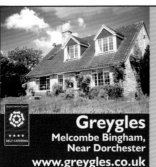
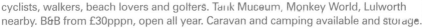

Visit the FHG website
www.holidayguides.com
for details of the wide choice of accommodation
featured in the full range of FHG titles

CALIFORNIA BARN Swanage BH19 2RS
Tel: 01929 425049 • Fax: 01929 421695
e-mail: delahays@hotmail.com • www.californiacottage.co.uk

A 200-year-old stone barn set in 11 acres of lush meadows with stunning sea views. The beautiful Jurassic Coast, recently designated a World Heritage Site, and the South West Coast Path lie only two fields away. Swanage, with all its family facilities is only one mile away. Converted and furnished to a high standard, the three bedrooms and three bathrooms can accommodate up to 10. The location of one bedroom and one bathroom on the ground floor make it ideal for wheelchair users and those with limited mobility. Visitors also have access to a large studio/meeting room. Arts tuition, wildlife and archaeological talks/tours can be arranged. No smoking. Pets allowed; livery available.

Short breaks available September to June (excl. Christmas and New Year).
£275-£575 for 3/4 nights • £475-£1000 per week

Peace and Tranquillity
Small select park with stunning views over Jurassic Coastline

GORSELANDS CARAVAN PARK
West Bexington-on-Sea, Dorset

- Excellent beach fishing
- Pets Welcome • Caravans & Apartments
- Camping nearby mid July-August • Shop and Launderette
- Village Pub 100 yards • Beach and car park one mile

SILVER

Tel: 01308 897232 • Fax: 01308 897239
www.gorselands.co.uk
e-mail: info@gorselands.co.uk
West Bexington-on Sea,
Near Bridport, Dorset DT2 9DJ

English Tourism Council
★★★★ HOLIDAY PARK

Grade II ListedCottage with 3 bedrooms, 2 bathrooms, approx. one minute walk to beach, close to harbour.

VB ★★★

Other properties available weekly or short breaks.

Weymouth has a lovely sandy beach and picturesque harbour with pavement cafes. There is plenty to do all year round.

Phone: 01305 836495 • Mobile: 0797 1256160
e-mail: postmaster@buckwells.plus.com
www.holidaycottageweymouth.co.uk
www.holidaycottagesweymouth.co.uk

symbols

 Totally non-smoking   Pets Welcome

 Children Welcome   Christmas Breaks

 Suitable for Disabled Guests   Licensed

Gloucestershire

Parkview is a fine Regency guesthouse which stands in Cheltenham's nicest area, only 10 minutes' walk from the centre. The bedrooms are large and airy and have TV, tea, coffee and provide views onto Pittville Park. Cheltenham is famous for horse racing and festivals of music and literature, and two theatres provide a regular programme of entertainment.

Nearby Prestbury is the most haunted village in England, the Cotswold villages stand in the surrounding hills, and Stratford is one hour's drive.

Parkview Guesthouse

**4 Pittville Crescent,
Cheltenham GL52 2QZ
Tel: 01242 575567
e-mail: stay@parkviewguesthouse.me.uk
www.parkviewguesthouse.me.uk**

Fairford, Parkend, Stow-on-the-Wold, Stroud

Your perfect retreat

Orion Holidays

The Cotswold Waterpark is an area of lakes larger than the Norfolk Broads. It offers a peaceful and attractive location for a tranquil countryside break. Our properties are ETC 4/5★ standard, many accept pets and sleep from 2-8 people.

Isis Lake: New England style lodges sit around the edge of the lake. All properties have an open plan living area with French doors leading out to your own private sundeck (many are lakeside). Isis offers a wide range of activities including fishing, tennis, children's play area, football and golf practice nets.

Spring Lake: All of the New England lodges sit along the edge of the lake and enjoy their own private lakeside south facing deck.
The lake offers a variety of watersports, children's play area, gym and a lakeside bar and brasserie.

Orion Holidays Ltd
The Gateway Centre, Lake 6, Spine Road East, South Cerney, Gloucestershire GL7 5TL
T: 01285 861839 • F: 01285 869188 • www.orionholidays.com

Isis Lake

Somerset

symbols

Totally non-smoking		Pets Welcome	
Children Welcome		Christmas Breaks	
Suitable for Disabled Guests		Licensed	

Wiltshire

The Old Bell Hotel
Abbey Row, Malmesbury
Wiltshire SN16 0BW
Tel: 01666 822344
www.oldbellhotel.com
info@oldbellhotel.com

Built in 1220 and reputed to be the oldest purpose-built hotel in England, **The Old Bell Hotel** is still offering quintessentially English warmth, comfort and hospitality nearly 800 years later.

Standing alongside Malmesbury's medieval Abbey, in England's first capital, the hotel provides outstanding levels of service and retains the ambience of a bygone age.

There are 33 en suite bedrooms, 18 in the main house, each furnished in an individual style, some with antique furniture, and a further 15 in the Coach House

- En suite facilities
- TV with DVD player and Freeview
- Wired broadband internet access.

Hayburn Wyke
GUEST HOUSE
★★★

Hayburn Wyke is a Victorian house, situated adjacent to Victoria Park, and a ten minute riverside walk from the city centre. Salisbury and surrounding area have many places of interest to visit, including Salisbury Cathedral, Old Sarum, Wilton House and Stonehenge. Most bedrooms have en suite facilities, all have television, and tea/coffee making equipment. Children are welcome at reduced rates. Sorry, no pets (guide dogs an exception). Private car parking for guests. Wi-Fi. Open all year. Credit cards and Switch accepted.

72 Castle Road, Salisbury SP1 3RL • Tel & Fax: 01722 412627
e-mail: hayburn.wyke@tinyonline.co.uk • www.hayburnwykeguesthouse.co.uk

Bed and full English Breakfast from £27

London & South East England

WITH A POPULATION of over seven million, London is by far the largest city in Europe, sprawling over an area of 620 square miles. For first-time visitors a city sight-seeing tour by double-decker bus or by boat along the River Thames is a 'must'. Even for those already familiar with the main attractions, there's always something new in London. Buckingham Palace is now open to the public and proving a very popular attraction. Visitors are welcome from the end of July to the end of September and can visit the magnificent State Apartments as well as the Queen's Gallery, which is open all year, displaying many Royal treasures.

A visit to London is not complete without seeing the new Docklands – an 8½ square mile area with a fantastic range of old and new architecture (including Britain's tallest building), pubs and restaurants, shops, visitor attractions and parks – all just a short journey from the City Centre.

With its orchards, hopfields, bluebell woods and vineyards it's not surprising that Kent is known as 'The Garden of England'. Historic Kent towns like Canterbury, Rochester and Broadstairs are a contrast with Dover, still the busiest passenger seaport in Europe and gateway to the Channel Tunnel.

The South East has many and varied resorts, including Brighton, with its two piers, prom, graceful Georgian houses, antique shops, and the famous Royal Pavilion, built at the request of the Prince of Wales, later Prince Regent and George IV. Eastbourne is another fine family resort, while in the quieter nearby town of Bexhill, low tides reveal the remains of a forest – part of the land bridge by which Britain was joined to Europe 10,000 years ago.

Seaside towns also cluster along the Hampshire coast around the port of Southampton, itself a picturesque town. And in the extreme east of the county is Portsmouth, a town irrevocably tied to its seafaring heritage. There are naval museums and ships to see, including Nelson's famous flagship from Trafalgar, The Victory.

www.enjoyengland.com
www.visitlondon.com
www.visitsoutheastengland.com

London & South East England
Great Days Out: Visits and Attractions

The Cartoon Museum
London • 020 7580 8155
www.cartoonmuseum.org
Just a stone's throw from The British Museum, The Cartoon Museum exhibits the very finest examples of British cartoons, caricature, and comic art from the 18th century to the present day.

BA London Eye
London • 0870 5000 600 www.londoneye.com
The world's highest observation wheel offers unrivalled views over London and beyond on its 30-minute slow-moving flight.

London Zoo• Gorilla Kingdom
London • 020 7722 3333
www.zsl.org
A brand new enclosure which is home to a colony of Western Lowland gorillas and colobus monkeys. Explore the forest pathways and then see these magnificent creatures in a natural clearing, surrounded by water.

The Living Rainforest
Near Newbury, Berkshire • 01635 202444
www.livingrainforest.org
Experience the sights, sounds and smells of a rainforest under glass. Gift shop, cafe.

Waddesdon Manor (NT)
Near Aylesbury, Bucks • 01296 653226
www.waddesdon.org.uk
A French Renaissance-style chateau housing the Rothschild Collection of art treasures. Superb gardens, aviary, restaurants, gift shops.

Bluereef Aquarium
Portsmouth, Hants • 023 9287 5222
www.bluereefaquarium.co.uk
The ultimate undersea safari. See the spectacular coral reef housed within a giant ocean display with its amazing walk-through tunnel.

Hollycombe Steam Collection
Liphook, Hants • 01428 724900
www.hollycombe.co.uk
Unique collection of working steam-powered attractions, including Edwardian fairground.

Seaview Wildlife Encounter
Seaview, Isle of Wight • 01983 612261
www.flamingoparkiw.com
A world of wildlife awaits you at this award-winning park with its hand-on programme of events that has something for everyone - excitement, adventure, entertainment and education.

Dickens World
Chatham, Kent • 01634 890421
www.dickensworld.co.uk
A fascinating journey through the life and works of the famous author. Experience the sights, sounds and smells of the 19th century.

Eagle Heights
Eynsford, Kent • 01322 866577
www.eagleheights.co.uk
One of the UK's largest bird of prey centres with over 50 species of raptors. Daily flying demonstrations, and collection of reptiles and mammals.

Didcot Railway Centre
Didcot, Oxfordshire • 01235 817200
www.didcotrailwaycentre.org.uk
A unique collection of Great Western Railway steam engines, coaches, wagons, buildings and small relics; and a recreation of Brunel's broad gauge railway.

Brooklands Museum
Weybridge, Surrey • 01932 857381
www.brooklandsmuseum.com
A history of aviation and motoring over the last 100 years, based at the original motor racing circuit. Try the Concorde Experience for yourself.

Ashdown Forest Llama Park
Near Forest Row, East Sussex • 01825 712040
www.llamapark.co.uk
A working farm where visitors can see breeding herds of llamas and alpacas. 'Walking with Llamas' - booking essential; large gift shop.

Weald & Downland Open Air Museum
Chichester, West Sussex • 01243 811363
www.wealddown.co.uk
Over 40 historic buildings carefully re-constructed, including medieval farmstead, working flour mill, and Victorian rural school.

London
(Central & Greater)

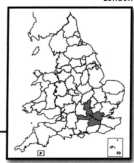

The Athena

110-114 SUSSEX GARDENS, HYDE PARK, LONDON W2 1UA

Tel: 0207 706 3866; Fax: 0207 262 6143

E-Mail: athena@stavrouhotels.co.uk   www.stavrouhotels.co.uk

TREAT YOURSELVES TO A QUALITY HOTEL AT AFFORDABLE PRICES

The Athena is a newly completed family run hotel in a restored Victorian building. Professionally designed, including a lift to all floors and exquisitely decorated, we offer our clientele the ambience and warm hospitality necessary for a relaxing and enjoyable stay. Ideally located in a beautiful tree-lined avenue, extremely well-positioned for sightseeing London's famous sights and shops; Hyde Park, Madame Tussaud's, Oxford Street, Marble Arch, Knightsbridge, Buckingham Palace and many more are all within walking distance.

Travel connections to all over London are excellent, with Paddington and Lancaster Gate Stations, Heathrow Express, A2 Airbus and buses minutes away.
Our tastefully decorated bedrooms have en suite bath/shower rooms, satellite colour TV, bedside telephones, tea/coffee making facilities. Hairdryers, trouser press, laundry and ironing facilities available on request. Car parking available.

Stavrou Hotels is a family-run group of hotels.
We offer quality and convenience at affordable rates.

A VERY WARM WELCOME AWAITS YOU.

Single Rooms from £50-£89

Double/Twin Rooms from £64-£99

Triple & Family Rooms from £25 per person

All prices include full English breakfast plus VAT.

Our hotels accept all major Credit cards, but some charges may apply.

 # Gower Hotel

129 SUSSEX GARDENS, HYDE PARK, LONDON W2 2RX
Tel: 0207 262 2262; Fax: 0207 262 2006
E-Mail: gower@stavrouhotels.co.uk   www.stavrouhotels.co.uk

The Gower Hotel is a small family-run Hotel, centrally located, within two minutes' walk from Paddington Station, which benefits from the Heathrow Express train "15 minutes to and from Heathrow Airport".

Excellently located for sightseeing London's famous sights and shops, Hyde Park, Madame Tussaud's, Oxford Street, Harrods, Marble Arch, Buckingham Palace and many more close by.

All rooms have private shower and WC, radio, TV (includes satellite and video channels), direct dial telephone and tea and coffee facilities. All recently refurbished and fully centrally heated. 24 hour reception.

All prices are inclusive of a large traditional English Breakfast & VAT

Discount available on 3 nights or more if you mention this advert

Stavrou Hotels is a family-run group of hotels.
We offer quality and convenience at affordable rates.
A VERY WARM WELCOME AWAITS YOU.

Single Rooms from £30-£79
Double/Twin Rooms from £60-£89
Triple & Family Rooms from £80

Our hotels accept all major Credit cards, but some charges may apply.

 # Queens Hotel

33 Anson Road, Tufnell Park, LONDON N7 0RB

Tel: 0207 607 4725; Fax: 0207 697 9725

E-Mail: queens@stavrouhotels.co.uk   www.stavrouhotels.co.uk

The Queens Hotel is a large double-fronted Victorian building standing in its own grounds five minutes' walk from Tufnell Park Station. Quietly situated with ample car parking spaces; 15 minutes to West End and close to London Zoo, Hampstead and Highgate. Two miles from King's Cross and St Pancras Stations. Many rooms en suite.

All prices include full English Breakfast plus VAT.
Children at reduced prices. Discounts on longer stays

Stavrou Hotels is a family-run group of hotels.
We offer quality and convenience at affordable rates.
A VERY WARM WELCOME AWAITS YOU.

Single Rooms from £30-£55
Double/Twin Rooms from £40-£69
Triple & Family Rooms from £20 per person

Our hotels accept all major Credit cards,
but some charges may apply.

Buckinghamshire

The Five Arrows Hotel
Waddesdon, Near Aylesbury, Buckinghamshire HP18 0JE
Tel: 01296 651727 • Fax: 01296 658596
e-mail: five.arrows@nationaltrust.org.uk • www.thefivearrows.co.uk

This charming small country hotel and restaurant stands at the gates of Waddesdon Manor. It was originally built by Baron Ferdinand de Rothschild to house the craftsmen and architects working on the Manor. There are nine en suite bedrooms and two suites. The bar and restaurant are open seven days a week. Lunch or dinner is a relaxed, informal experience, and on fine days may be enjoyed in the pretty courtyard and garden. It has a reputation for imaginative modern European food, with a wine list featuring a wide range of Rothschild wines.

Open for breakfast, morning coffee, lunch, afternoon tea and dinner
Sunday lunches are served from 12 noon to 7pm • Children welcome

Lymington, Lyndhurst

Hampshire

symbols

 Totally non-smoking   Pets Welcome

 Children Welcome   Christmas Breaks

 Suitable for Disabled Guests   Licensed

New Forest Ponies

Photo courtesy of Hampshire County Council

Isle of Wight

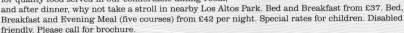

Totland Bay, Yarmouth

Kent

Sandwich, Tenterden

symbols

Totally non-smoking	Pets Welcome
Children Welcome	Christmas Breaks
Suitable for Disabled Guests	Licensed

Oxfordshire

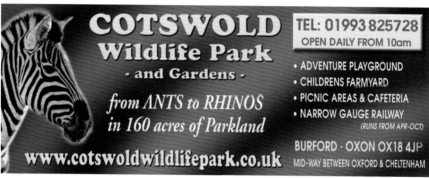
Oxford

Readers are requested to mention this FHG
guidebook when seeking accommodation

Surrey

The Hurtwood Inn Hotel

Set at the heart of the picturesque village of Peaslake, in the beautiful Surrey Hills, this family-run, privately owned hotel has an enviable reputation for the individuality and quality of its cuisine and hospitality

Ideally placed to explore some of England's finest countryside, such as Leith Tower Hill, South of England's highest point with breathtaking views, the National Trust properties of Polesden Lacey and Clandon Park, and nearby the historic county town of Guildford.

Hotel of the Year • Millenium South East England Tourist Board Award 2000 (under 50 bedrooms)

21 tastefully furnished en suite bedrooms. 'Oscars' Restaurant with superb local reputation, serving modern and traditional cuisine in the intimate dining room.

Hurtwood Inn Hotel, Walking Bottom, Peaslake, Near Guildford, Surrey GU5 9RR
Tel: 01306 730851 • Fax: 01306 731390
e-mail: sales@hurtwoodinnhotel.com • www.hurtwoodinnhotel.com

Please note

LYTHE HILL
HOTEL & SPA

Nestled deep within the Surrey countryside the Four Star Lythe Hill Hotel and Spa is a unique and very special venue, where traditional values of hospitality and service meet with the opulence and ease of modern facilities.

- Award-Winning Restaurant
- 41 Beautifully Furnished Bedrooms and Suites
- Fourteenth Century Tudor House
- Extensive Conference and banqueting Facilities
- Civil Marriages and Wedding Facilities

- Amarna – Health, Beauty & Fitness Spa
- Sauna, Steam room and Cold Temple Shower
- Wide range of luxurious Beauty Treatments
- Fully eqipped techno gym with Cardio Theatre

Special weekend leisure breaks available inclusive of 3 course à la carte dinner, accommodation, full English breakfast and full use of the Amarna Spa facilities.

Lythe Hill Hotel & Spa, Petworth Road, Haslemere, Surrey, GU27 3BQ
t: **01428 651 251**   e: lythe@lythehill.co.uk   www.lythehill.co.uk

---

Chase Lodge Hotel
An Award Winning Hotel
with style & elegance, set in tranquil surroundings
at affordable prices
10 Park Road Hampton Wick Kingston-Upon-Thames KT1 4AS
Tel: 020 8943 1862 . Fax: 020 8943 9363
E-mail: info@chaselodgehotel.com Website:www.chaselodgehotel.com
Quality en suite bedrooms and
Full Buffet Continental Breakfast www.surreyhotels.com

Licensed bar
Wedding Receptions
Honeymoon suite
available with jacuzzi & steam area
20 minutes from Heathrow Airport
Close to Kingston town centre & all
major transport links.

★★★   All major credit cards accepted

Visit the FHG website
www.holidayguides.com
for details of the wide choice of accommodation

featured in the full range of FHG titles

East Sussex

The Powder Mills is a privately owned 18thC Listed country house hotel in 150 acres of beautiful parklands, woods and lakes, adjoining the famous battlefield of 1066. Once a famous gunpowder mill, it has been skilfully converted into a fascinating country hotel. The Orangery Restaurant, with its marble floor, Greek statues and huge windows looking out onto the terrace and pool, has been awarded an AA Rosette for fine dining. There is a range of 40 individually decorated en suite bedrooms and Junior Suites, many with 4-poster beds. The Pavilion is a delightful conference centre, accommodating up to 200 persons, situated away from the main hotel with its own parking facilities, and suitable also for concerts, events and weddings. The Powder Mills is open to non-residents every day for luncheon, light lunches and dinner.

Powder Mills Hotel & The Orangery Restaurant
Powdermill Lane, Battle TN33 0SP • Tel: 01424 775511
www.powdermillshotel.com • e-mail: powdc@aol.com

symbols

 Totally non-smoking

 Children Welcome

 Suitable for Disabled Guests

 Pets Welcome

 Christmas Breaks

 Licensed

Chiddingly, Eastbourne

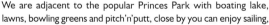

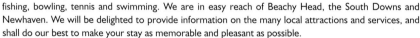

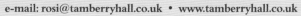

Rye,

West Sussex

East of England

Photo courtesy of Essex County Council

EAST ANGLIA, once a Saxon kingdom cut off from the rest of England by marshland and forest, remains to this day a relatively unexplored part of Britain. It is an area of low, chalky hills, pleasant market towns, working windmills adding charm to the fields, wide sweeping views over the flattest land and glorious sunsets. Along East Anglia's North Sea coast, the visitor can choose between bustling seaside resorts or long stretches of deserted sandy beaches. Boating enthusiasts come from all over the world for holidays afloat on the Norfolk Broads, an ancient man-made network of shallow tree-fringed lakes, rivers and canals. East Anglia's inland towns are full of history and proud to tell their stories at visitor centres and museums. Specialist museums abound. The Imperial War Museum at Duxford Airfield has the largest collection of military and civil aircraft in Britain. Duxford was a Battle of Britain station and the flatness of East Anglia gave it the wartime distinction of having the largest number of airfields in the country. Steam, vintage and miniature railway museums, classic car collections, bicycle museums: East Anglia has them all, as well as the famous Lace Museum (with magnifying glasses provided) in Norfolk, a Working Silk Museum at the restored silk mills in Braintree, and a Motorboat Museum in Basildon tracing the history of motor boats, racing hydroplanes and leisure boats. At Lowestoft harbour you can step aboard the last survivor of more than 3000 drifters that came every autumn to Yarmouth and Lowestoft, following the plentiful shoals of herring. Visual displays portray the hardships of the herring workers, male and female, who brought prosperity to the two ports for more than a century but only poverty to themselves. It was a different way of life – above stairs at least – for the inhabitants of the great mansion houses of East Anglia in their heyday. The Queen's favourite country seat in England, Sandringham House, is open to the public from the end of July to the end of October.

www.visiteastofengland.com

East of England
Great Days Out: Visits and Attractions

Whipsnade Zoo
Dunstable, Bedfordshire • 01582 872171
www.zsl.org/whipsnade
See rare and endangered species from around the world. Visitors can take a trip through the Woodland Bird Walk and visit the children's farm in 600 acres of parkland. New Cheetah Rock.

Linton Zoo
Linton, Cambridgeshire • 01223 891308
www.lintonzoo.co.uk
The emphasis is on conservation and education. with lots of rare and exotic animals. Set in 16 acres of beautiful gardens, with picnic and children's play areas.

Colne Valley Railway
Castle Hedingham, Essex • 01787 461174
www.colnevalleyrailway.co.uk
Take a ride on an award-winning country railway. Visitor Centre and new Garden Railway; regular 'Days Out with Thomas the Tank Engine'.

Knebworth House
Near Stevenage, Herts • 01438 812661
www.knebworthhouse.com
Home of the Lytton family since 1490, with fine collections of manuscripts, portraits and furniture. Set in 250 acre country park with formal gardens and large adventure playground. Gift shop, cafe.

Hatfield House
Hatfield, Herts • 01707 287010
www.hatfield-house.co.uk
Jacobean house built by the Cecil family. Rich in paintings, furniture, tapestries and armour. Extensive gardens, recently restored.

Sandringham
Near King's Lynn, Norfolk • 01553 612908
www.sandringham-estate.co.uk
The Queen's country estate – 600 acres of gardens and lakes; house and museum of royal vehicles also open to public.

Pettitts Animal Adventure Park
Near Great Yarmouth, Norfolk • 01493 700094
www.pettittsadventurepark.co.uk
Three parks in one - fun for all the family. Rides, play area, adventure golf course, animals galore.

Merrivale Model Village
Great Yarmouth, Norfolk • 01493 842097
www.greatyarmouthmodelvillage.co.uk
Model village set in an acre of landscaped gardens - watch out for the bank robber and the streaker! New Merrival Castle. Tea room and shop.

Dinosaur Adventure Park
Lenwade, Norwich, Norfolk • 01603 876310
www.dinosaurpark.co.uk
Follow the Dinosaur Trail and meet giants from the past. Make friends with animals, from hedgehogs to wallabies, bugs and snakes, in the secret animal garden.

National Horse Racing Museum
Newmarket, Suffolk • 01638 667333
www.nhrm.co.uk
Five permanent galleries tell the story of the development of the "sport of kings" over 400 years. Meet retired jockeys and ride the horse simulator.

Kentwell Hall & Gardens
Long Melford, Suffolk • 01787 310207
www.kentwell.co.uk
A lovely Elizabethan house, brought back to life as a unique family home. Award-winning re-creations of everyday life in Tudor and WWII times. Gardens, rare breeds farm, maze, plus lots more.

East Anglia Transport Museum
Near Lowestoft, Suffolk • 01502 518459
www.eatm.org.uk
A wide range of historic vehicles including trams, trolleybuses, motor buses, steam rollers, cars, lorries and taxis. There is also a 2ft-gauge railway. Visitors can ride on many of the vehicles and also view the period street furniture.

Bedfordshire

symbols

Totally non-smoking			Pets Welcome
Children Welcome			Christmas Breaks
Suitable for Disabled Guests			Licensed

Norfolk

Visit the FHG website

www.holidayguides.com

for details of the wide choice of accommodation

featured in the full range of FHG titles

symbols

Totally non-smoking		Pets Welcome	
Children Welcome		Christmas Breaks	
Suitable for Disabled Guests		Licensed	

FHG Guides
publish a large range of well-known accommodation guides.
We will be happy to send you details or you can use the order form
at the back of this book.

Much more than just quality holidays.

Searles
LEISURE RESORT
•HUNSTANTON•
2009

Relaxing, excellent value for money beauty spa breaks out of the school holidays, ideal for a group of friends.

Reflections Hair and Beauty Salon at Searles

Included in Our Beauty Spa package are the following:

- Unlimited use of the Indoor Pool, Sauna, Jacuzzi and Gymnasium.
- Two days Half Board including Evening meals and Breakfast.
- Full access to all of Searles' superb leisure and entertainment facilities.
- Choose 4 treatments from a list of 12 different options.

Our beauty breaks cost just £98 per person.

Just add your choice of accommodation to the package price. Other additional treatments can be purchased at a discount off the tariff price.

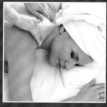

Accommodation

Searles accommodation is available in eight different ranges, from luxurious pine lodges to Classic Cabins, cosy Coastal Cottages, to the inviting Royal Range; we have something to suit all tastes.

Our Leisure Lodges, Prestige & Winchester Range represent real quality in terms of furniture, fixtures, size and setting, in fact all of the comforts of home with those special added extras to make any stay a real pleasure.

Tel: (01485) 534211
visit us at **www.searles.co.uk**

Call our friendly booking team today!

Searles Leisure Resort, South Beach, Hunstanton, Norfolk PE36 5BB

REF: FHG

Winterton-on-Sea

Winterton Valley Holidays

A selection of modern superior fully appointed holiday chalets in a choice of locations near Great Yarmouth. Enjoy panoramic views of the sea from WINTERTON, a quiet and picturesque 35-acre estate minutes from the beach, while CALIFORNIA has all the usual amenities for the more adventurous holidaymaker, with free entry to the pool and clubhouse. Pets very welcome at both sites.

For colour brochure please ring 01493 377175 or write to 15 Kingston Avenue, Caister-on-Sea, Norfolk NR30 5ET • www.wintertonvalleyholidays.co.uk

Suffolk

Saxtead

Our beautiful lodges are nestled around our small fishing lake in peaceful countryside. Each lodge features a secluded hot tub on the veranda - the perfect place to relax! Guests have use of indoor, heated swimming pool and fishing in private lake. Individually furnished to a high standard, with dishwasher, cooker, fridge, microwave etc in the kitchen. Lounges feature large comfy sofas, TV, DVD, video and stereo. Full central heating throughout. Veranda overlooking lake with barbecue and patio furniture. Sleep 2 -8.

WINDMILL LODGES Red House Farm, Saxtead, Woodbridge IP13 9RD
Tel: 01728 685338 • Fax: 01728 684850
e-mail: holidays@windmilllodges.co.uk • www.windmilllodges.co.uk

Please note

All the information in this book is given in good faith in the belief that it is correct. However, the publishers cannot guarantee the facts given in these pages, neither are they responsible for changes in policy, ownership or terms that may take place after the date of going to press. Readers should always satisfy themselves that the facilities they require are available and that the terms, if quoted, still apply.

Felixstowe

ROUND OFF A
PERFECT DAY

Enjoy a break on the invigorating Heritage Coast. Play the challenging, mature 18-hole seaside course designed by the legendary James Braid. Guests in the hotel can enjoy concessionary rates at Aldeburgh Golf Club, one of the top 100 courses in the British Isles or play the Suffolk Tour including Ipswich, Woodbridge and Felixstowe Ferry. A warm welcome, comfortable en suite rooms and good food.

The Thorpeness Hotel, Thorpeness, Aldeburgh, Suffolk IP16 4NII
Tel: 01728 452176 • Fax: 01728 453868
e-mail: info@thorpeness.co.uk • www.thorpeness.co.uk

A beautiful Tudor mansion set in the heart of the Suffolk countryside, this outstanding country hotel gazes out over sweeping lawns to a picturesque lake. For an invigorating break from routine, this has it all: peerless accommodation, a magnificent cuisine, style, and a captivating aura of living history. Pretty fabrics and tasteful decor set off contemporary luxuries to maximum advantage, and en suite guest rooms of all sizes are superbly appointed. In the dining room exquisitely prepared dishes are presented amidst a setting of glassware, gleaming silver and spotless napery, with a mouth-watering vegetarian selection also on offer. The Courtyard Leisure Club, set inside the adjacent Tudor tithe barn, includes a large swimming pool, spa bath, fully equipped gymnasium and beauty salon.

SECKFORD HALL HOTEL

Woodbridge, Suffolk IP13 6NU
Tel: 01394 385678 • Fax: 01394 380610
e-mail: reception@seckford.co.uk
www.seckford.co.uk

Visit the FHG website
www.holidayguides.com
for details of the wide choice of accommodation
featured in the full range of FHG titles

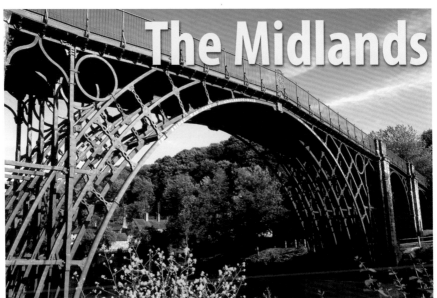

The Midlands

Ironbridge   Photo courtesy of Shropshire County Council

FOLLOWING The Romantic Road is not what immediately comes to mind when the English Midlands are being considered as a holiday destination. Nevertheless, the Romantic Road is a very suitable title for a guide to the picture-postcard villages of the Cotswolds which is available from Cheltenham Tourism. The gentle hills and honey-coloured houses of the Cotswolds are deservedly popular with tourists in summer. Quieter, but just as beautiful in their way, are other scenic areas of the Midlands: the Wye Valley, the Vale of Evesham, Sherwood Forest, once the haunt of the legendary Robin Hood and, near the Welsh border, the wooded valleys known as the Marches around the towns of Hereford and Shrewsbury

In a secluded valley in this area a discovery was made that changed the face of the world when Abraham Darby perfected his revolutionary techniques for the mass production of cast iron. Today there are no fewer than seven museums in the Gorge, which has been designated a World Heritage Site.

To keep the children happy there is also a Teddy Bear Museum and the Ironbridge Toy Museum. Children are welcome at the Heritage Motor Centre at Gaydon, the largest collection of British cars in the world; quad biking over rough terrain track is available for children.

Staffordshire is the home of the Potteries and some of the best china and porcelain in the world is made there. Visit Stoke-on-Trent for the complete China Experience, factory tours, ceramic museums and, to take home as a souvenir of the Midlands, world famous names like Wedgwood, Royal Doulton and Spode china at amazing discounts.

www.visitheartofengland.com
www.enjoyenglandseastmidlands.com

The Midlands
Great Days Out: Visits and Attractions

Crich Tramway Museum
Crich, Derbyshire • 01773 852565
www.tramway.co.uk
Nestling high up in the heart of Derbyshire overlooking the famous Derwent Valley, Crich Tramway Village is a lovingly restored period village that is also home to the National Tramway Museum and its world renowned archives.

Eastnor Castle
Near Ledbury, Herefordshire • 01531 633160
www.eastnorcastle.com
Fairytale Georgian Castle dramatically situated in the Malvern Hills in an area of outstanding natural beauty and surrounded by a deer park, arboretum and lake. Beautifully restored interiors contain medieval armour, tapestries and Italian fine art.

Conkers – National Forest Centre
Moira, Leicestershire • 01283 216633
www.visitconkers.com
Award-winning attraction at the heart of the National Forest. Explore the woodland trails, relax by the lakeside. Woodland garden, adventure playground, restaurant and shop.

Holdenby House
Northampton, Northants • 01604 770074
www.holdenby.com
This stately home was built by Sir Christopher Hatton and became the Palace of James I. Now a family home, the house is the splendid backdrop to a beautiful garden and Falconry Centre.

Natural World Centre
Near Lincoln, Lincolnshire • 01522 688868
www.naturalworldcentre.com
Our Changing World exhibition, eco-friendly shopping, walks through wildlife haven. Lots of special events, workshops, children's activities.

Acton Scott Historic Working Farm
Church Stretton, Shropshire • 01694 781306
www.shropshire.gov.uk/museums
Practical demonstrations of traditional country skills with visits from the farrier, wheelwright and blacksmith. Waymarked walks, friendly animals, shop with country crafts, cafe.

Blackbrook Zoological Park
Near Leek, Staffs • 01538 308293
www.blackbrookzoo.co.uk
Many unusual species of birds, including storks and cranes. Children's farm, pets' area, insect and reptile house. New for 2008 - Meet the Penguins.

Heritage Motor Centre
Gaydon, Warwickshire • 01926 641188
www.heritage-motor-centre.co.uk
The largest collection of British veteran, vintage and classic cars in the world. 4-wheel drive demonstration circuit, children's roadway, cafe and gift shop.

Stratford-upon-Avon Butterfly Farm
Stratford-upon-Avon, Warwickshire
01789 299288 • www.butterflyfarm.co.uk
Hundreds of free-flying exotic butterflies in a natural jungle setting. Visit Insect City with leaf-cutting ants, giant millipedes and lots more - all safely behind glass!

Coventry Transport Museum
Coventry, West Midlands • 024 7623 4270
www.transport-museum.com
The largest display in the world of British-made road transport, from buses to bikes. Tiatsa Model Collection, Coventry Blitz Experience and lots more.

Thinktank at Millennium Point
Birmingham • 0121 202 2222
www.thinktank.ac
10 themed galleries help us understand how science and technology shape our lives. You can examine the past, investigate the present and explore what the future may bring.

Avoncroft Museum
Near Bromsgrove, Worcs • 01527 831363
www.avoncroft.org.uk
Historic buildings saved from destruction, including a working windmill, furnished houses and the National Telephone Kiosk Collection.

Derbyshire

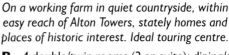

symbols

 Totally non-smoking

 Children Welcome

 Suitable for Disabled Guests

 Pets Welcome

 Christmas Breaks

 Licensed

Belmont, Hereford, Leominster

Herefordshire

Oakham

Leicestershire & Rutland

BARNSDALE LODGE HOTEL

A delightful, welcoming country house hotel situated between the north shore of Rutland Water and The Earl of Gainsborough's Exton Park Estate. An ideal base to visit Geoff Hamilton's Barnsdale Gardens, Belton House (National Trust), Burghley House and the historic market towns of Stamford and Oakham with all the attractions of Rutland Water; sailing, windsurfing, fishing, cycling and beautiful scenic walks. A bistro menu based on locally sourced produce is served in relaxed surroundings of the dining room, conservatory or courtyard garden. Viclente beauty treatment room now open. This excellent accommodation comprises rooms with en suite bathrooms, Sky television, broadband, radio alarms, and tea/coffee making facilities. Children's menu - cots available. Pets welcome. Private gardens.

The Avenue, Rutland Water, North Shore, Near Oakham, Rutland LE15 8AH
Tel: 01572 724678 • Fax: 01572 724961 • e-mail: enquiries@barnsdalelodge.co.uk
www.barnsdalelodge.co.uk　　　*ETC ★★★ and Silver Award • AA ★★★*

FHG Guides

publish a large range of well-known accommodation guides.
We will be happy to send you details or you can use the order form
at the back of this book.

symbols

Totally non-smoking		Pets Welcome
Children Welcome		Christmas Breaks
Suitable for Disabled Guests		Licensed

Lincolnshire

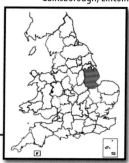

Louth, Market Rasen, Skegness, Sutton-on-Sea

Northamptonshire

Visit the FHG website
www.holidayguides.com

for details of the wide choice of accommodation

featured in the full range of FHG titles

symbols

	Totally non-smoking		Pets Welcome
	Children Welcome		Christmas Breaks
	Suitable for Disabled Guests		Licensed

Shropshire

Ludlow

Staffordshire

Stoke-on-Trent

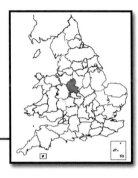

The only spa resort in a stately home in England. This graceful residence has been restored to its former glory and offers a unique combination of traditional elegance and first class service, along with with the extensive facilities of a modern spa resort - two swimming pools, three saunas, three steam rooms, water grottos, aerobics, yoga, a 4000 sq ft gymnasium, tennis and golf. There is a choice of over 100 beauty treatments and therapies designed to ease the aches and pains of modern living. Tasty cuisine is a top priority, with two restaurants to choose from. Accommodation is in the luxury class, and includes spacious superior and master bedrooms, as well as suites and penthouses for the ultimate in pampering.

Voted England's Leading Resort for 4 consecutive years at the World Travel Awards.

HOAR CROSS HALL
SPA RESORT

Hoar Cross, Near Yoxall,
Staffordshire DE13 8QS
Tel: 01283 575671
info@hoarcross.co.uk
www.hoarcross.co.uk

Looking for Holiday Accommodation?

for details of hundreds of properties throughout the UK, visit our website

www.holidayguides.com

Warwickshire

Worcestershire

Eckington

The North of England

Blackpool

Photo courtesy of Blackpool Council

THERE ARE SOME PEOPLE who prefer a holiday where every day is packed with action and every evening filled with fun. Others see a holiday as the exact opposite, a chance to get some peace and quiet in the wide open spaces. Whatever sort of holidaymaker you are, the North of England has plenty to offer you. The North has some of the best living museums and 'hands-on' visitor centres in Britain, where the latest presentation techniques are equally fascinating to adults and children. How does the world look to a fish, a dog, a bee? Find out – and learn to make rainbows too – at the Colour Museum in the once-grimy city of Bradford. Also in Bradford is the National Media Museum which has Britain's biggest cinema screen, a thousand times bigger than your TV screen at home – and not content with that, it also has the world's only Cinerama cinema, the world's biggest lens, smallest camera and first-ever photographic likeness! Just as interesting are the smaller heritage museums to be found in practically every town and village in the North. Britain's National Railway Museum is in York, the birthplace of the steam railway. If a day trip behind a steam engine is more your style, ask for the Yorkshire Tourist Board's leaflet 'Steaming Along' with details of seven steam railways and the dates of the kiddies' specials – the Thomas the Tank Engine week-ends.

The seaside resorts of the North have provided happiness for children and relaxation for Mums and Dads for generations. In Lancashire, on the west coast, Southport, St Annes, Blackpool, Morecambe – often it's the same resort families choose year after satisfied year. The twin resorts of Whitley Bay and Tynemouth are on the North Tyneside coast. From bright lights to walking on the fells, from heritage visits to Sunday shopping, you'll find them all in the North of England!

www.golakes.co.uk
www.visitnortheastengland.com
www.visitenglandsnorthwest.com
www.yorkshire.com

North of England
Great Days Out: Visits and Attractions

Hat Works
Stockport, Cheshire • 0845 8330975
www.hatworks.org.uk
In a restored Grade II Listed Victorian mill, the UK's only museum dedicated to hats and headwear. Demonstrations of working machinery, AV shows, and an extensive collection of hats. Family Fun area, guided tours.

Trotters World of Animals
Bassenthwaite, Cumbria • 017687 76239
www.trottersworld.com
Award-winning wildlife park set amidst picturesque Lakeland fells, with a full programme of activities throughout the year. Indoor and outdoor play areas; picnic area.

Cumberland Pencil Museum
Keswick, Cumbria • 017687 73626
www.pencilmuseum.co.uk
The fascinating history of the humble pencil, from the discovery of Borrowdale graphite to present day manufacture. See the world's largest colouring pencil. Shop.

Killhope Lead Mining Museum
Near Cowshill, Co Durham • 01388 537505
www.durham.gov.uk/killhope
Get a glimpse of a vanished way of life with a trip to Park Level Mine, and a re-creation of the appalling working and living conditions of the late 19th century. A real 'hands on' adventure which brings the past vividly to life.

National Football Museum
Preston, Lancashire• 01772 908442
www.nationalfootballmuseum.com
The story of the world's greatest game. In two distinctive halves, it can be enjoyed by supporters of all ages. Shop and restaurant.

Knowsley Safari Park
Prescot, Merseyside • 0151 430 9009
www.knowsley.com
Around 30 species of mammal roaming 200 hectares of land. Also Children's Lake Farm, the Bug House, sealion shows, miniature railway, amusement park rides and bird of prey displays.

Alnwick Castle
Alnwick, Northumberland • 01665 511100
www.alnwickcastle.com
Famous as Hogwarts School in the Harry Potter films. Visit the Knights School and Alnwick Garden, with its huge Treehouse and Poison Garden.

Centre for Life
Newcastle, Tyne & Wear • 0191-243 8210
www.life.org.uk
The secret of life – how it works, what it means. A thrilling motion-simulator ride, live theatre, 3D interactive exhibits, virtual reality – an unforgettable experience.

Eden Camp Modern History Museum
Malton, North Yorkshire • 01653 697777
www.edencamp.co.uk
This award-winning museum will take you back to wartime Britain where you can experience the sights, sounds and smells of World War II.

Magna Science Adventure Centre
Rotherham, South Yorkshire • 01709 720002
www.visitmagna.co.uk
The UK's first Science Adventure Centre explores the four elements of Fire, Earth, Air and Water. Experience sound and light shows, fire giant water cannons, and lots more!

The Deep
Hull, South Yorkshire • 01482 381000
www.thedeep.co.uk
A journey from the beginning of time telling the story of the oceans, using a combination of hands-on activities, AV presentations and living exhibits.

National Media Museum
Bradford, West Yorkshire • 0870 7010200
www.thedeep.co.uk
Journey through popular photography, visit IMAX, discover the past, present and future of television in Experience TV, watch your favourite TV moments in TV Heaven, play with light, lenses and colour in the Magic Factory and explore the world of animation and watch a real animator at work in the Animation Gallery.

East Yorkshire

symbols

 Totally non-smoking

 Children Welcome

 Suitable for Disabled Guests

 Pets Welcome

 Christmas Breaks

 Licensed

North Yorkshire

symbols

	Totally non-smoking		Pets Welcome
	Children Welcome		Christmas Breaks
	Suitable for Disabled Guests		Licensed

Skipton

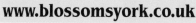

ST GEORGE'S
6 St George's Place,
York YO24 1DR
Tel: 01904 625056
Fax: 01904 625009
e-mail: sixstgeorg@aol.com
www.stgeorgesyork.com

St George's is a small and friendly family-run Victorian residence in a quiet cul-de-sac by York's beautiful racecourse.

- All rooms, one of which is on the ground floor, are en suite with tea/coffee tray and TV. • Non-smoking.
- Vegetarians are catered for. • Private enclosed parking.
- The hotel is only a 10-minute walk from the City Walls and many places of historic interest.
- £60 per double or twin room

ST. GEORGE'S

Wortley

South Yorkshire

West Yorkshire

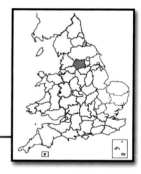

Wakefield

Northumberland

symbols

 Totally non-smoking

 Children Welcome

 Suitable for Disabled Guests

 Pets Welcome

 Christmas Breaks

 Licensed

WAREN LEA HALL
Waren Mill, Bamburgh
Luxurious Self-Catering
Holiday Accommodation
for families, parties and friends.

Near Bamburgh on the beautiful coast of Northumberland.

Standing on the shore of beautiful Budle Bay, an Area of Outstanding Natural Beauty and a Site of Special Scientific Interest for its birdlife, lies spectacular WAREN LEA HALL. This lovely, gracious old Hall, set in 2 ½ acres of shoreline parkland and walled gardens, enjoys breathtaking views across the bay and sea to Lindisfarne. In addition to THE HALL there are two entirely self-contained apartments, GHILLIE'S VIEW and GARDEN COTTAGE..

THE HALL *(for up to 14 guests)*

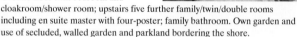

Beautifully furnished to complement its Edwardian grandeur, with high ceilings, chandeliers, sash windows, fireplaces and polished wooden floors. Breathtaking views from every room. Large drawing and dining rooms opening on to floodlit terrace; large, fully equipped kitchen/breakfast room. Ground floor twin bedroom and cloakroom/shower room; upstairs five further family/twin/double rooms including en suite master with four-poster; family bathroom. Own garden and use of secluded, walled garden and parkland bordering the shore.

GARDEN COTTAGE *(for up to 4 guests)*

The terrace wing of Waren Lea Hall, reached through its own entrance from the garden. All the light and sunny rooms are prettily furnished with high quality fabrics, pine furniture and polished wooden floors throughout, and face the lovely gardens which guests can use. The well equipped kitchen/dining room, lounge, double and twin bedrooms, one en suite, and family shower room are all on one level.

GHILLIE'S VIEW *(for up to 10 guests)*

The former home of the estate ghillie, accommodation is all on one level, with luxurious furnishings throughout. Fully equipped kitchen/dining room, semi-circular drawing room and master bedroom with four-poster and en suite shower; all with fine views across the river and bay to Holy Island. Double and twin rooms, one en suite, and family shower room Guests have use of walled garden and parkland.

For further information please contact the owners:
Carolynn and David Croisdale-Appleby
Abbotsholme, Hervines Road
Amersham, Buckinghamshire HP6 5HS
Tel: 01494 725194 • Mobile: 07901 716136
e-mail: croisdaleappleby@aol.com
www.selfcateringluxury.co.uk

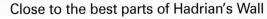

Please note

RIVERDALE HALL HOTEL

Bellingham, Hexham, Northumberland NE48 2JT

Riverdale Hall Hotel lies on the banks of the North Tyne salmon river, on the outskirts of the small market town of Bellingham, Northumberland. With southerly views over its own cricket field, and Dunterley Fell (part of the Pennine Way), it is situated in the hilly and rugged fells of the Northumberland National Park. Nearby are Kielder Water and Kielder Forest, and of course Hadrian's Wall. This is indeed walking, fishing and sporting country.

Built in 1866, the present owners, the Cocker family, have tastefully converted it into one of Northumbria's most outstanding Country House Hotels.

All hotel bedrooms at Riverdale Hall are well appointed with en suite bathrooms, shower, colour television, telephone, and tea and coffee making facilities. Some of the bedrooms are equipped with luxurious four-poster beds, whilst others are designated as family rooms, and can accommodate additional beds as required.

Riverdale Hall has its own large indoor heated pool and sauna, which is open all year round and is freely available to our residents.

The Riverdale Hall Hotel's elegantly appointed restaurant provides a warm relaxed setting for enjoying a meal and a bottle of wine from our extensive wine list. Award-winning cuisine, complemented by friendly and efficient service, adds up to a delightful gourmet experience.

The restaurant has received a Les Routiers Gold Plate Award (the only hotel in Northumbria to receive this accolade), numerous AA rosettes, RAC blue ribbons and been named the "Best Hotel in Northumberland."

There are also five self-catering units available.

Tel: 01434 220254

e-mail:
reservations@riverdalehallhotel.co.uk

www.riverdalehallhotel.co.uk

Iben (Head Chef) and John Cocker receive the Les Routiers Gold Plate Award from Clarissa Dickson Wright (Two Fat Ladies) and Sir John Scott.

The Cocker Family's 31st year

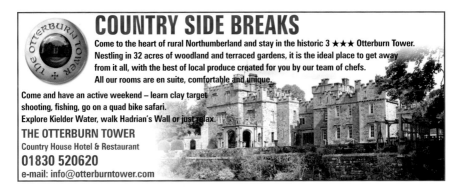

Cheshire

Jo and Pete Hollins offer guests a friendly welcome to their home on a 145-acre working farm in quiet and peaceful surroundings. Green Farm is situated on the Cheshire/Staffordshire border and is within easy reach of Junction 16 on the M6. An excellent stop-over place for travellers journeying between north and south of the country.

Two double en suite and two twin en suite in converted cottage can be either B&B or self-catering using the fully equipped kitchen in the cottage, all on ground floor. B&B from £25pp.
• *Tea-making facilities and TV in all rooms* • *Cot provided*
• *Pets welcome* • *Open all year* • *Caravans and tents welcome*

This area offers many attractions; we are within easy reach of historic Chester, Alton Towers and the famous Potteries of Staffordshire.

Mrs Joanne Hollins,
Balterley Green Farm, Deans Lane,
Balterley, Near Crewe CW2 5QJ
Tel: 01270 820214

The Curzon Hotel • Chester

This attractive Victorian town house hotel is situated just a stone's throw from the many attractions of this historic city.

• 16 en suite bedrooms, all with TV, tea/coffee making, hairdryer and telephone. Doubles, twins and large family rooms available, also Four-poster Suites, all non-smoking.

• Candlelit restaurant overlooking pretty gardens. Monthly-changing menus offer the finest in British and international cuisine. Carefully selected wine list.

Special breaks are a feature of The Curzon Hotel, whether you are looking for a weekend in a Chester hotel or a romantic getaway.

52-54 Hough Green, Chester CH4 8JQ
Tel: 01244 678581 • Fax: 01244 680866
www.curzonhotel.co.uk

Deva Breaks available all year round, any 2 nights or more DB&B
Romantic Breaks • Winter Warmers

---

symbols

Ambleside

Cumbria

Ferndale Lodge is a small, family-run guesthouse close to the centre of Ambleside, where you will find a warm and friendly welcome. Offering excellent accommodation at realistic prices with a hearty home cooked English or Vegetarian breakfast. All 10 bedrooms have full en suite facilities, colour television and tea/coffee making tray. Full central heating throughout, rooms available with fell views, including a ground floor bedroom. The Ferndale is open all year round with a private car park, offers packed lunches, clothes/boot drying and ironing facilities. A wide choice of places to dine are within minutes of a level walk. An ideal walking base. Special offers available, please telephone for more details.

Bed and Breakfast £25-£35pppn. Weekly £175-£210pp. Please phone for brochure.

Ferndale Lodge, Lake Road, Ambleside LA22 0DB
Tel: 015394 32207
e-mail: stay@ferndalelodge.co.uk www.fern-dalelodge.co.uk

★★★
GUEST HOUSE

Ambleside Lodge

Heart of the English Lake District. This elegant Lakeland home, dating from the 19th century, has been sympathetically converted and now offers a high standard of accommodation. All bedrooms are en suite, with colour TV, tea/coffee making facilities and delightful views. The Premier suites and king-size four-poster rooms with jacuzzi spa baths offer relaxation and indulgence. Leisure facilities available at a private club just 5 minutes' drive away include swimming pool, sauna, steam room, squash, gym and beauty salon.

www.ambleside-lodge.com

AMBLESIDE LODGE, ROTHAY ROAD, AMBLESIDE, CUMBRIA LA22 0EJ
015394 31681 • Fax: 015394 34547 • e-mail: enquiries@ambleside-lodge.com

Greenhowe Caravan Park
Great Langdale, English Lakeland.

Greenhowe is a permanent Caravan Park with Self Contained Holiday Accommodation. Subject to availability Holiday Homes may be rented for short or long periods from 1st March until mid-November. The Park is situated in the heart of the Lake District some half a mile from Dungeon Ghyll at the foot of the Langdale Pikes. It is an ideal centre for Climbing, Fell Walking, Riding, Swimming, or just a lazy holiday.

Please ask about Short Breaks.

NEW LODGES THIS YEAR

Greenhowe Caravan Park

Great Langdale, Ambleside
Cumbria LA22 9JU

For free colour brochure
Telephone: (015394) 37231
Fax: (015394) 37464
www.greenhowe.com

Ambleside, Bassenthwaite

Bowness-on-Windermere, Coniston, Grange-over-Sands

Grange-over-Sands, Hawkshead, Keswick

symbols

⊘ Totally non-smoking
🐴 Children Welcome
♿ Suitable for Disabled Guests

🐕 Pets Welcome
✧ Christmas Breaks
♈ Licensed

SEACOTE PARK

The Beach, St Bees,
Cumbria CA27 0ET
Tel: 01946 822777
Fax: 01946 824442
reception@seacote.com
www.seacote.com

Adjoining lovely sandy beach on fringe of Lake District, modern luxury holiday caravans for hire, fully equipped to sleep up to 8. Full serviced touring pitches and tent area. St Bees is convenient for touring, with Ennerdale, Eskdale and Wasdale, plus some of England's finest mountain scenery within easy reach. Holiday caravans also for sale.

Tarnside Caravan Park
5 miles from St Bees, own tarn where fishing is available

Seven Acres Caravan Park
small park set among the trees just outside Gosforth

Silloth-on-Solway

Tanglewood Caravan Park

CAUSEWAY HEAD, SILLOTH-ON-SOLWAY, CUMBRIA CA7 4PE

TANGLEWOOD is a family-run park on the fringes of the Lake District National Park. It is tree-sheltered and situated one mile inland from the small port of Silloth on the Solway Firth, with a beautiful view of the Galloway Hills. Large modern holiday homes are available from March to January, with car parking beside each home. Fully equipped except for bed linen, with end bedroom, panel heaters in bedrooms and bathroom, electric lighting, hot and cold water, toilet, shower, gas fire, fridge and colour TV, all of which are included in the tariff. Touring pitches also available with electric hook-ups and water/drainage facilities, etc. Play area. Licensed lounge with adjoining children's play room. Pets welcome free but must be kept under control at all times. Full colour brochure available. **AA THREE PENNANTS ★★★**

TEL: 016973 31253 • e-mail: tanglewoodcaravanpark@hotmail.com • www.tanglewoodcaravanpark.co.uk

• DOWNLOADABLE BROCHURE WITH TARIFF AND BOOKING FORM AVAILABLE ON WEBSITE. •

An ideal base from which to explore this beautiful part of the country, for those seeking quality food and care in a warm and friendly atmosphere.

22 comfortably furnished en suite bedrooms, all with colour TV, radio, direct-dial telephone and hospitality tray.

Restaurant • Lounge Bar • Snooker Room
Games Room • Residents' Lounge
Championship links at Silloth-on-Solway Golf Club; many other clubs nearby.

GOLF HOTEL, SILLOTH-ON-SOLWAY CA7 4AB • Tel: 016973 31438
Fax: 016973 32582 • e-mail: info@golfhotelsilloth.co.uk • www.golfhotelsilloth.co.uk

Looking for Holiday Accommodation?

for details of hundreds of properties throughout the UK, visit our website

www.holidayguides.com

Windermere

symbols

 Totally non-smoking

 Children Welcome

 Suitable for Disabled Guests

 Pets Welcome

 Christmas Breaks

 Licensed

Lancashire

THE BROWN LEAVES COUNTRY HOTEL

LONGSIGHT ROAD, COPSTER GREEN,
NEAR BLACKBURN BB1 9EU
Tel: 01254 249523 • Fax: 01254 245240

Whether visiting on business or travelling en route to the Lake District or the Yorkshire Dales, everyone in search of comfortable reasonably priced en suite hotel accommodation need look no further than The Brown Leaves Country Hotel. Set in impressive and extensive grounds, all guests are assured of the warmest of welcomes with every attention given to their comfort and overall satisfaction.

All accommodation is conveniently situated at ground floor level. Your en suite room is well furnished, with matching bed linen and curtains in addition to remote-control satellite colour television, hairdryer, trouser press, free wireless internet and beverage making facilities.

Dinner available Monday to Thursday inclusive. Home-style cooking at its finest, varied in choice and superbly presented. Comfortable lounge bar with good selection of beers, lagers and fine wines. Tranquil garden with views towards Longridge Fell and the Ribble Valley. Choice of breakfast including vegetarian is served in the spacious dining room.

Everything at The Brown Leaves Country Hotel is offered in a genuinely friendly manner and with an understated air of quality. The perfect base from which to visit a number of notable beauty spots.
Special Discounts when quoting this guide.

www.brownleavescountryhotel.co.uk

FHG Guides
publish a large range of well-known accommodation guides.
We will be happy to send you details or you can use the order form
at the back of this book.

THE
CHADWICK HOTEL
South Promenade, Lytham St Annes FY8 1NP

Owned and run by the Corbett family since 1947, the Chadwick Hotel commands a delightful seafront position overlooking the Ribble Estuary, just five miles from Blackpool and conveniently situated for touring the Lake District, Manchester, the Yorkshire Dales and North Wales.

The friendly atmosphere and modern facilities encourage guests to return again and again.

The Bugatti Bar is cosy and relaxed, while the Four Seasons Restaurant offers a classically elegant atmosphere in which to enjoy quality food and service.

All 75 bedrooms are en suite, some with spa baths, others with four-poster beds.
Open throughout the year, the hotel also boasts a luxurious health and leisure complex.

FACILITIES INCLUDE: Family rooms, a soft play adventure area, games room, baby listening and launderette. Children can have high tea or dinner with their parents. A special Children's Menu features a selection of children's favourites. Children sharing family rooms – less than half adult rate. Babies in cots FREE of charge. 24 hour food and drinks service. Night porter. Ample parking.

Tel: 01253 720061 • Fax: 01253 714455
www.thechadwickhotel.com
sales@thechadwickhotel.com

AA
★★★
HOTEL

★★★
HOTEL

The Fylde Coast's Favourite Family Hotel

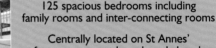

125 spacious bedrooms including family rooms and inter-connecting rooms

Centrally located on St Annes' famous promenade and sandy beach

With fabulous leisure facilities including 20 metre pool

Free crèche and family entertainment during weekends and school holidays*

subject to availability

Full range of speciality teas, coffees, snacks and light meals Perfect for a pit stop Sun terrace Free wireless internet
Open 9am-6pm mon-thur
9am-7pm fri & sat

A modern menu influenced by classics from Britain and the Mediterranean using local produce.
Open every evening from 6pm
www.atrium-restaurant.co.uk

Gymnasium with separate Cardio Theatre, Pool, Jacuzzi, Sauna, Aromatic Steam Room Kids weekend fitness and funky dance classes Awarded North West Decleor Aroma Gold Spa of the Year Quality treatments and total relaxation.

t:01253 712236
w:www.dalmenyhotel.co.uk
e:reservations@dalmenyhotel.co.uk
Dalmeny Hotel & Leisure, South Promenade, St Annes on Sea, Lancashire, FY8 1LX

dalmeny HOTEL & LEISURE

Scotland • Regions

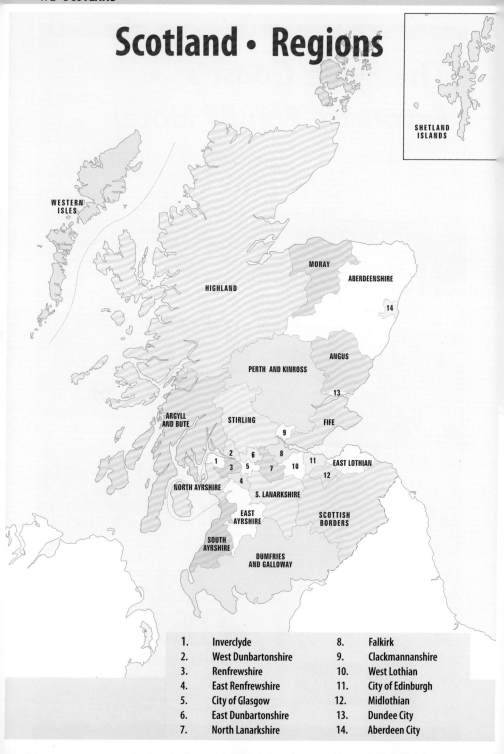

SHETLAND
ISLANDS

WESTERN
ISLES

MORAY

ABERDEENSHIRE

HIGHLAND

14

ANGUS

PERTH AND KINROSS

13

ARGYLL
AND BUTE

STIRLING

FIFE

9

2

6

8

1

5

7

10

11

EAST LOTHIAN

3

4

12

NORTH AYRSHIRE

S. LANARKSHIRE

EAST
AYRSHIRE

SCOTTISH
BORDERS

SOUTH
AYRSHIRE

DUMFRIES
AND GALLOWAY

1.	Inverclyde	8.	Falkirk
2.	West Dunbartonshire	9.	Clackmannanshire
3.	Renfrewshire	10.	West Lothian
4.	East Renfrewshire	11.	City of Edinburgh
5.	City of Glasgow	12.	Midlothian
6.	East Dunbartonshire	13.	Dundee City
7.	North Lanarkshire	14.	Aberdeen City

Scotland

Caolasnacon Caravan & Camping Park, Kinlochleven, p186

Glenan Lodge. Tomatin, Highlands, p210

Ardbrecknish House, by Dalmally, Argyll, p184

THE HIGHLANDS AND ISLANDS include much of what is often thought of as the 'real' Scotland. Stretching north from Fort William and Ben Nevis in the west to Inverness and the Moray Firth in the east, this unspoiled area contains some of Britain's most remote, least populated and most beautiful districts. The North West Highlands is the first area of Scotland to be awarded UNESCO-endorsed European Geopark status. The area which encompasses parts of Wester Ross and the whole of North West Sutherland has been designated as a Geopark on the basis of its outstanding geology and landscape, the strength of its partnership approach to sustainable economic development and its existing geological interpretation.

On the eastern borders of the Highlands lie Aberdeenshire and Moray, with their rugged peaks and rolling farmlands. Rich in fish, whisky, oil and castles, these counties boast 'Royal' Deeside, with Braemar and Balmoral as a tourist 'honeypot' and share with their neighbouring counties some of the most impressive scenery in Britain. Perth & Kinross and Angus offer a wealth of leisure activities: ski-ing in the glens, fishing on Loch Leven or Loch Earn, golf at Gleneagles or Carnoustie, climbing Lochnagar, pony trekking round Loch Tay, or sea-bathing at Arbroath or Montrose. The many attractive towns like Pitlochry, Aberfeldy, Crieff, Forfar etc and the busy cities of Perth and Dundee offer civilised shopping, eating and accommodation facilities.

Convenient road, rail and air links make Central and South-West Scotland a popular tourist destination. Argyll has a long, much indented coastline, looking out onto a scatter of islands such as Mull, Jura, Gigha and Islay. This is a popular outdoor resort area and has excellent hotels and a wide choice of self catering accommodation. Oban is the principal centre and a busy port for the Inner and Outer Hebrides. The lively city of Glasgow is well worth a visit and has a growing reputation for its superb cultural, entertainment, shopping and sporting facilities. Ayrshire naturally means Rabbie Burns and Alloway, and also means golf – Prestwick, Troon and Turnberry are courses of international renown. Make time for a trip across to the lovely Isle of Arran – 'Scotland in miniature'.

Central Scotland is surprisingly rich in scenery and historic interest. The 'bonnie banks' of Loch Lomond, the Trossachs, Stirling Castle and Bannockburn are just some of the treasure stored here in the heart of Scotland. Excellent holiday centres with plenty of accommodation include Stirling itself, Killin, Aberfoyle, Callander, Lochearnhead and Dunblane. The rolling hills and fields of the Lothians, with Edinburgh at the heart, sweep down to the Forth as it enters the North Sea.

Edinburgh is the country's capital and a year-round tourist destination. It is always full of interest – the castle, the Palace of Holyrood, museums, galleries, pubs and entertainment. North Berwick and Dunbar are popular coastal resorts and this area, like Fife and Ayrshire, is a golfers' paradise. Opening onto the sea between the Lothians and Berwick-on-Tweed (which is technically in England), are the very attractive Scottish Borders. The ruined abbeys of Dryburgh, Jedburgh, Kelso and Melrose are a main attraction, as are the mills and mill-shops for the woollens which have made towns like Hawick and Galashiels famous.

A short break in St Andrews and the Kingdom of Fife is the ideal escape from the pressures of everyday life. Curl up in a comfy chair by a roaring fire in an ancient castle hotel. Sample superb cuisine in gracious surroundings in a stately home. Or treat the family to a self-catering break in a house with a view. And no matter what time of year you choose to come, you can be sure that there will be plenty of things to see and do. With its dry climate, most sports, including golf, can be played throughout the year. And as the scenery changes character with each season, you will notice something new no matter how many times you return. It is, of course, golf that has placed Fife on the world stage. St Andrews is the "Home of Golf", and the town, and Fife in general, boasts many fine courses which can be played all year round.

For walkers, the Southern Upland Way runs from Cockburnpath on the east coast, through the Borders to Portpatrick, near Stranraer from where ferry services leave for Northern Ireland. We are now in Dumfries & Galloway whose hills and valleys run down to the Solway Firth within sight of the English Lake District. This is a popular touring and holiday region, with its green and fertile countryside, pleasant small towns and villages, and many attractions to visit.

www.visitscotland.com

Looking out from Birnam Hill, Perthshire   Photo courtesy of Perth & Kinross Council

Scotland
Great Days Out: Visits and Attractions

Culzean Castle and Country Park
Maybole, Ayrshire • 01655 884455
www.culzeanexperience.org
Robert Adam's masterpiece set in beautifully landscaped gardens. Investigate the Eisenhower connection and visit the Interpretation Centre, swan pond and aviary. Restaurant and tea rooms, picnic areas.

Creetown Gem Rock Museum
Newton Stewart, Dumfries & Galloway
01671 820357 • www.gemrock.net
Gems, crystals, rocks and fossils from all over the world, many displayed in a realistic cave setting; 'Fire in the Stones' AV presentation; tearoom and internet cafe.

Kelvingrove Art Gallery & Museum
Glasgow • 0141-276 9599
www.glasgowmuseums.com
An adventure through art, time and the natural world brought to life, with film, sound and computer activities in Glasgow's newly restored museum and art gallery.

Scottish Fisheries Museum
Anstruther, Fife • 01333 310628
www.scotfishmuseum.org
Situated on the harbour front in Anstruther, in the heart of the Fife fishing community, the Scottish Fisheries Museum tells the story of fishing in Scotland and its people, from earliest times to the present.

Sensation Science Centre
Dundee • 01382 228800
www.sensation.org.uk
A unique 4-star visitor attraction devoted to the five senses, with over 60 hands-on exhibits, live science shows and workshops.

Castle & Gardens of Mey
Near Thurso, Caithness • 01847 851473
www.castleofmey.org.uk
The most northerly castle on the British mainland, renovated and restored by the late Queen Mother. Beautiful gardens with views across the Pentland Firth to Orkney.

The Loch Ness Monster Visitor Centre
Drumnadrochit, Inverness • 01456 450342
www.lochness-centre.com
All you ever wanted to know about the monster! Superb documentary, including eye-witness accounts. Shop with souvenirs.

Our Dynamic Earth
Edinburgh • 0131 550 7800
www.dynamicearth.co.uk
Charting the Earth's progress and development over the last 4500 million years, with plenty of interactive entertainment to fascinate all ages.

National Museum of Flight
East Fortune Airfield, Lothians • 01620 897240
www.nms.ac.uk/museumofflight
Discover the extraordinary story of our human ambition to take to the skies. The hangars are packed with aircraft that reveal how flight developed from the Wright brothers to Concorde.

Scone Palace
Perth • 01738 552300
www.scone-palace.net
With a history stretching back 1500 years, this has been the seat of parliaments and the crowning place of kings. It is a treasury of furniture, paintings, porcelain and objets d'art. Adventure playground and maze.

The Falkirk Wheel
Falkirk, Stirlingshire • 08700 500 208
www.thefalkirkwheel.co.uk
Measuring 115ft. the world's only rotating boatlift links the Forth & Clyde and Union Canals using state-of-the-art engineering. Visitor centre and boat trips.

Blair Drummond Safari Park
By Stirling, Stirlingshire • 01786 841456
www.blairdrummond.com
Big animals in drive-through enclosures , plus pets farm, falconry displays and boat trips to chimpanzee island. Other activities for the kids include a flying fox (a wire suspended over the lake which brave souls can descend on!), pedal boats and a giant astraglide..

Ladyglen Hotels

Hetland Hall Hotel	King Robert Hotel	Rob Roy Hotel
Carrutherstown	Glasgow Road	Aberfoyle
Dumfries	Bannockburn	Stirlingshire
DG1 4JX	Stirling FK7 0LJ	FK8 3UX
Tel: 01387 840201	Tel: 01786 811666	Tel: 01877 382245
Fax: 01387 840211	Fax: 01786 811507	Fax: 01877 382262
info@hetlandhallhotel.co.uk	info@kingroberthotel.co.uk	info@robroyhotel.co.uk
www.hetlandhallhotel.co.uk	www.kingroberthotel.co.uk	www.robroyhotel.co.uk

Please note

All the information in this book is given in good faith in the belief that it is correct. However, the publishers cannot guarantee the facts given in these pages, neither are they responsible for changes in policy, ownership or terms that may take place after the date of going to press. Readers should always satisfy themselves that the facilities they require are available and that the terms, if quoted, still apply.

Aberdeen, Banff & Moray

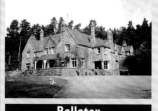

symbols

 Totally non-smoking

 Children Welcome

 Suitable for Disabled Guests

Pets Welcome

Christmas Breaks

Licensed

Visit the FHG website

www.holidayguides.com

for details of the wide choice of accommodation

featured in the full range of FHG titles

Angus & Dundee

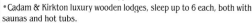

Glen Clova Hotel, Glen Clova, Near Kirriemuir DD8 4QS • Tel: 01575 550350
Fax: 01575 550292 • e-mail: Hotel@clova.com • www.clova.com

Set in an area of oustanding natural beauty and botanical interest, Glen Clova has something to offer everyone. Be our guest and live *The Real Scottish Experience.*

- All bedrooms with full en suite facilities, courtesy trays and TV.
- The Steading Bunkhouse provides basic but functional self-catering accommodation for the true outdoor type.
- Cadam & Kirkton luxury wooden lodges, sleep up to 6 each, both with saunas and hot tubs.
- Climbers' Bar with a lively atmosphere, fine cask ales and a roaring fire in winter; Lounge Bar and Conservatory offer comfortable, informal surroundings for relaxation.

Argyll & Bute

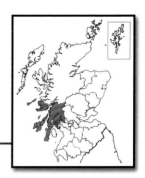

AA ★★★★   Scottish Tourist Board **★★★★ SMALL HOTEL**   🏆🏆🏆

THE ***Airds***
HOTEL & RESTAURANT

Port Appin, Appin, Argyll PA38 4DF
Tel: 01631 730236 • Fax: 01631 730535
e-mail: airds@airds-hotel.com • www.airds-hotel.com

For breathtaking mountain and loch views and a stupendous cuisine that is a gourmet's dream, this neat, tidy and homely hotel is an aesthetic delight. Flowers are everywhere, sitting rooms are hung with romantic, gold-framed prints, books fill alcoves and fires blaze and crackle all day long. Bedrooms are stylishly furnished and possess what can only be described as thoughtful niceties and some of the bathrooms are almost as large as the bedrooms they serve. Through gabled windows, the eye is enchanted by views of the distant mountains of Morvern, seemingly rising out of the sea. Walkers thrill to the possibilities of a varied terrain from rugged paths to strolls through carpets of wild flowers.

Scottish Tourist Board **★★★★ GUEST HOUSE**

AA ★★★★ Guest House

Lyn-Leven, a superior, award-winning licensed guest house overlooking Loch Leven, with every comfort, in the beautiful Highlands of Scotland, is situated one mile from historic Glencoe village.
Four double, two twin and two family bedrooms, all rooms en suite; sittingroom and diningroom. Central heating. Excellent and varied home cooking served daily. Children welcome at reduced rates. An ideal location for touring. Fishing, walking and climbing in the vicinity. The house is open all year except Christmas. Car not essential but private car park provided.
Bed and Breakfast from £25 • Dinner, Bed and Breakfast from £235 to £255 per person per week
Credit and debit cards accepted

Mr & Mrs J.A. MacLeod, Lyn-Leven Guest House, Ballachulish PH49 4JP
Tel: 01855 811392 • Fax: 01855 811600 • www.lynleven.co.uk

FHG Guides
publish a large range of well-known accommodation guides.
We will be happy to send you details or you can use the order form
at the back of this book.

www.holidayguides.com

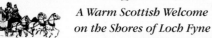

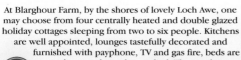

Situated in the Inner Hebrides, the community owned Isle of Gigha (God's Island) is surely one of Scotland's most beautiful and tranquil islands. Explore the white sandy bays and lochs. Easy walking, bike hire, birds, wildlife and wild flowers. Home to the famous Achamore Gardens with rhododendrons, azaleas and semi-tropical plants. Grass Airstrip, 9-hole golf course and regular ferry (only 20 minutes from the mainland). We are dog friendly. Holiday Cottages also available.

Call us on 01583 505254 Fax: 01583 505244 **www.gigha.org.uk**

CAOLASNACON
Caravan & Camping Park, Kinlochleven PH50 4RJ
There are 20 static six-berth caravans for holiday hire on this lovely site with breathtaking mountain scenery on the edge of Loch Leven — an ideal touring centre.
Caravans have electric lighting, Calor gas cookers and heaters, toilet, shower, fridge and colour TV. There are two toilet blocks with hot water and showers and laundry facilities. Children are welcome and pets allowed. Open from April to October. Milk, gas, soft drinks available on site; shops three miles. Sea loch fishing, hill walking and boating; boats and rods for hire, fishing tackle for sale.
www.kinlochlevencaravans.com
e-mail: caolasnacon@hotmail.co.uk

For details contact
Mrs Patsy Cameron - 01855 831279

Inchmurrin Island

SELF-CATERING HOLIDAYS

Inchmurrin is the largest island on Loch Lomond and offers a unique experience. Three self-catering apartments, sleeping from four to six persons, and a detached cedar clad cottage sleeping eight, are available.

The well appointed apartments overlook the garden, jetties and the loch beyond. Inchmurrin is the ideal base for watersports and is situated on a working farm.

Terms from £407 to £850 per week, £281 TO £560 per half week.

A ferry service is provided for guests, and jetties are available for customers with their own boats. Come and stay and have the freedom to roam and explore anywhere on the island.

e-mail: scotts@inchmurrin-lochlomond.com
www.inchmurrin-lochlomond.com
Inchmurrin Island,
Loch Lomond G63 0JY
Tel: 01389 850245 • Fax: 01389 850513

Kings Knoll Hotel

The hotel enjoys magnificent views standing in its own grounds overlooking Oban Bay and is the first hotel that visitors meet when entering on the A85. Most bedrooms are en suite with colour TV and hospitality tray. The elegant Kings Rest lounge bar has a Highland theme and is ideal for a cosy dram before dinner in the Knoll restaurant, which specialises in fresh local produce. Oban is ideally located for visiting the Western Isles and exploring the spectacular local scenery.

Dunollie Road, Oban PA34 5JH
Tel: 01631 562536 • Fax: 01631 566101
e-mail: info@kingsknollhotel.co.uk
www.kingsknollhotel.co.uk

West Loch Hotel

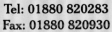

By Tarbert
Loch Fyne
Argyll
PA29 6YF

Tel: 01880 820283
Fax: 01880 820930

An attractive, family-run, 18th century coaching inn of character, the West Loch Hotel is well situated for a relaxing holiday. It is renowned for outstanding food. After dining, guests can relax in front of an open fire, perhaps sampling some of the local malt whiskies. With glorious scenery, the area is excellent for hill-walking and enjoying the wide variety of wildlife. Visits to Islay, Jura, Arran and Gigha can be pleasant day trips, and attractions in the area include castles, distilleries, gardens and sandy beaches. Fishing, golf and boat hire are all available locally.

www.westlochhotel.co.uk • westlochhotel@btinternet.com

symbols

  Totally non-smoking   Pets Welcome

  Children Welcome   Christmas Breaks

  Suitable for Disabled Guests   Licensed

Ayrshire & Arran

Ayr, Prestwick

We look forward to welcoming you to Craig Holm Guest House. Our friendly, family-run Victorian beachfront townhouse boasts modern fresh decor, great facilities incl. wifi, and spectacular views along the coastline. We are just 4.1 miles from Glasgow Prestwick Airport, with good road, rail & bus links; perfect for business travellers, sport/leisure breaks, peaceful weekend getaways or touring around Scotland.

Golf, one of the area's major attractions, brings tens of thousands of visitors each year. We are within 30 minutes' drive of all Ayrshire's top courses, including the world class Royal Troon, Turnberry, Prestwick St Nicholas & Western Gailes.

7 Queens Terrace, Ayr KA7 1DU • Tel: 01292 261470 • Fax: 0808 280 1029
e-mail: craigholmayr@aol.com • www.craigholmayr.com

North Beach
Hotel
5-7 Links Road, Prestwick KA9 1QG
Tel: 01292 479069
Fax: 01292 671521
info@northbeach.co.uk
www.northbeach.co.uk

• Overlooking 'Old Prestwick' golf course
• Many of our rooms have spectacular views over the famous links
• Equipped with every modern comfort
• The perfect base from which to tour first-class Ayrshire courses
• Our restaurant has a locally envied reputation for excellent cuisine.

Open all year • Single from £45, Double/Twin from £85

Please note
All the information in this book is given in good faith in the belief that it is correct. However, the publishers cannot guarantee the facts given in these pages, neither are they responsible for changes in policy, ownership or terms that may take place after the date of going to press. Readers should always satisfy themselves that the facilities they require are available and that the terms, if quoted, still apply.

THE CARLTON HOTEL

The Carlton Hotel in Prestwick is easily accessible to Ayrshire's finest golf courses including the Championship courses, Old Prestwick, Troon and Turnberry, which are just a short drive away. Prestwick International Airport is located 1.5 miles from the hotel, with Glasgow International Airport 40 miles away.

A warm welcome awaits guests at the hotel, which offers a Carvery Restaurant, with a choice of quality carved meats and fresh market vegetables, freshly prepared starters, main course alternatives, sweet options and a wide range of refreshments. Comfortable lounge areas provide guests with a relaxing environment to enjoy a welcome beverage from the bar after a busy day exploring the west coast of Scotland.

A choice of double/twin and family en suite accommodation is available within the 40 newly refurbished en-suite bedrooms.

The Carlton Hotel, 187 Ayr Road, Prestwick KA9 1TP
Tel: 01292 476811 • www.carlton-prestwick.com
e-mail: reception@carlton-prestwick.com

South Beach Hotel

Troon, Ayrshire KA10 6EG
Tel: 01292 312033 • Fax: 01292 318438
e-mail: info@southbeach.co.uk
www.southbeach.co.uk

★Privately-owned hotel, facing the sea.
★Easy reach of 15 quality courses.
★Golf club store and drying facilities.
★Golf packages to suit your requirements.
★32 en suite bedrooms (suites available).
★Enjoy your golf break in a happy, friendly atmosphere. ★Phone for details.

A useful index of towns/counties appears on pages 236-238

FHG Guides

publish a large range of well-known accommodation guides.
We will be happy to send you details or you can use the order form
at the back of this book.

Borders

The Green, Denholm
Near Hawick TD9 8NU
01450 870305
Karen & Dave

The **Auld Cross Keys** Inn
www.crosskeysdenholm.co.uk

The Inn enjoys an exceptional reputation in the area for good food and excellent ales. Accommodation is available in seven bedrooms (6 en suite, one with private bathroom), all with TV, hairdryer and hospitality tray. The inn is a popular venue for weddings and other functions, and is ideally situated for golfing breaks in the Scottish Borders.

Golf • Fishing • Walking

Ferniehirst Mill Lodge

Built in 1980, Ferniehirst Mill Lodge has all the amenities required for your comfort whilst blending with the existing mill buildings and stables. Just south of Jedburgh, situated in a secluded valley, the Lodge is a haven for bird life. Ideal for walking, fishing and horse riding. 8 bedrooms, all with en suite bathroom or shower, and tea and coffee making facilities. Central heating throughout and the spacious lounge has a log fire for chillier evenings. Full cooked breakfast and dinner are served in the attractive pine dining room. The emphasis is on home cooking using local produce. There is a small bar for residents. *Personal service and warm hospitality from owners Alan and Christine.*

Jedburgh TD8 6PQ
Tel: 01835 863279

ferniehirstmill@aol.com • www.ferniehirstmill.co.uk

AA
★★
Guest House

Dumfries & Galloway

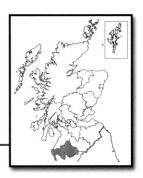

Visit the FHG website

www.holidayguides.com

for details of the wide choice of accommodation

featured in the full range of FHG titles

Edinburgh & Lothians

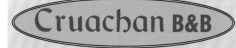

A relaxed and friendly base is provided at Cruachan from which to explore central Scotland. The centre of Edinburgh can be reached by train in only 30 minutes from nearby Bathgate, and Glasgow is only 35 minutes by car.

All rooms en suite/private facilities, full hospitality tray, fresh towels daily, colour TV and central heating. Hosts Kenneth and Jacqueline ensure you receive the utmost in quality of service, meticulously presented accommodation and of course a full Scottish breakfast. They look forward to having the pleasure of your company.

Bed and Breakfast from £29 per person per night.

78 East Main Street, Blackburn EH47 7QS
Tel: 01506 655221 • Fax: 01506 652395
e-mail: cruachan.bb@virgin.net
www.cruachan.co.uk

MARTIN'S GUEST HOUSE
5 Granville Terrace, Edinburgh EH10 4PQ
Tel: 0131 229 2086

Martin's is ideally situated within easy walking distance of all Edinburgh's main attractions.
We offer a warm welcome, lots of local knowledge, personal service, comfortable rooms and delicious breakfasts.
Family rooms available • Private car parking.
Good nearby bus services • B&B from £20-£45pppn

Short Breaks £68pp for 3 nights (sharing en suite room)
October-April (subject to availability)

e-mail: info@martinsguesthouse.co.uk • www.martinsguesthouse.co.uk

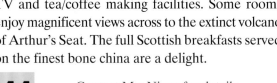

Fife

Lower Largo, Lundin Links

symbols

    Totally non-smoking

    Pets Welcome

    Children Welcome

    Christmas Breaks

    Suitable for Disabled Guests

    Licensed

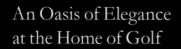

An Oasis of Elegance
at the Home of Golf

Fairmont St Andrews, Scotland
St Andrews, Fife, KY16 8PN
T: 01334 837000 F: 01334 471115
www.fairmont.com/standrews

Highlands

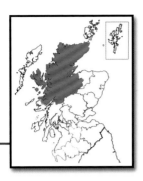

Royal Marine Hotel
Brora, Sutherland KW9 6QS

Charming Robert Lorimer Highland retreat overlooking the River Brora and adjacent James Braid's famous golf course. Excellent food, fine wines and roaring log fires! Leisure Club with pool. Comfortable rooms, choice of formal dining in Lorimer's room or informally in the Bistro or Garden Room. Great location to explore the north or golf at Royal Dornoch.

"The Links" Apartments
Brora, Sutherland KW9 6QS

Contemporary sleep 4 en suite luxury apartments with stunning views over James Braid's famous course. Breathtaking miles of unspoiled beaches. A great place to chill out, read a book or write one! Full use of the Royal Marine Hotel's Leisure club and extensive food and beverage facilities or simply self-cater.

Drumnadrochit, Fort William

Loch Ness   Photo courtesy of Wilderness Cottages, Errogie, Inverness

Invermoriston, Nairn, Spean Bridge

Glenan Lodge

is a typical Scottish Lodge situated in the midst of the Monadhliath Mountains in the valley of the Findhorn River, yet only one mile from the A9. It offers typical Scottish hospitality, home cooking, warmth and comfort.

The seven bedrooms, including two family rooms, are all en suite, with central heating, tea-making facilities and colour TV.

AA
★★★
Guest Accommodation

There is a large comfortable lounge and a homely dining room. The licensed bar is well stocked with local malts for the guests.

Glenan Lodge caters for the angler, birdwatcher, hillwalker, stalker and tourist alike whether passing through or using as a base.

• Bed and Breakfast; Dinner optional • Credit cards accepted •
• Non-smoking • Open all year round •

Robert Coupar & Lesley Smithers, Glenan Lodge (Licensed),
Tomatin IV13 7YT • Tel & Fax: 0845 6445793
e-mail: enquiries@glenanlodge.co.uk • www.glenanlodge.co.uk

Borgie Lodge Hotel

Skerray, Tongue, Sutherland KW14 7TH

Set in a secluded Highland glen by the stunning River Borgie lies Borgie Lodge, where mouthwatering food, fine wine, roaring log fires and a very warm welcome await after a day's fishing, hill walking, pony trekking or walking on the beach. Relax after dinner with a good malt and tales of salmon, trout and deer.

Scottish TOURIST BOARD ★★★★ HOTEL

AA
★★
⊛

Tel: 01641 521 332
www.borgielodgehotel.co.uk
e-mail: info@borgielodgehotel.co.uk

FHG Guides

publish a large range of well-known accommodation guides.
We will be happy to send you details or you can use the order form
at the back of this book.

www.holidayguides.com

Lanarkshire

symbols

Totally non-smoking		Pets Welcome
Children Welcome		Christmas Breaks
Suitable for Disabled Guests		Licensed

Perth & Kinross

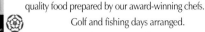

FHG Guides
publish a large range of well-known accommodation guides.
We will be happy to send you details or you can use the order form
at the back of this book.

A useful index of towns/counties appears on pages 196-198

Tayside Hotel

• Hotel • Bar • Restaurant • Function Rooms •

Warm hospitality and delicious home cooked cuisine: A wonderful short break destination as well as a home from home for an extended Scottish vacation

Come and stay in one of our 14 en-suite guest rooms for a short break or a longer escape. While you're with us try your hand at some local activities including Salmon Fishing, Golf, River Rafting or Highland Safaris.... sample a wee dram at one of the many local whisky distilleries.... or simply take it slow and enjoy some of the beautiful Perthshire landscape.

All Rooms Twin or Double En-Suite
Bed and Breakfast or Half Board basis available
Dogs Welcome

Mill St, Stanley, Perthshire PH1 4NL
www.tayside-hotel.co.uk   reception@tayside-hotel.co.uk   01738 82 82 49

This 330 acre farm is situated on the A9, six miles north of Perth. Accommodation comprises twin and double en suite rooms and a family room with private bathroom; lounge, sittingroom, diningroom; bathroom, shower room and toilet. Bed and Breakfast from £25. The warm welcome and supper of excellent home baking is inclusive. Reductions and facilities for children. Pets accepted. Ample car parking. Excellent local restaurants nearby. The numerous castles and historic ruins around Perth are testimony to Scotland's turbulent past. Situated in the area known as "The Gateway to the Highlands" the farm is ideally placed for those seeking some of the best unspoilt scenery in Western Europe. Many famous golf courses and trout rivers in the Perth area.

Newmill Farm, Stanley PH1 4QD
Mrs Ann Guthrie • 01738 828281

e-mail: guthrienewmill@sol.co.uk
www.newmillfarm.co.uk

Looking for Holiday Accommodation?

FHG
·K·U·P·E·R·A·R·D·

for details of hundreds of properties throughout the UK, visit our website
www.holidayguides.com

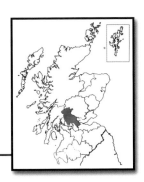

Stirling & The Trossachs

Scottish Islands

the albert hotel

Luxury rooms in the centre of Kirkwall
Contemporary Orkney style
Relaxing atmosphere
Cosy Bothy Bar
Orkney ales and whiskies
Variety of dining options
Great local produce

telephone: 01856 876000   fax: 01856 875397
e-mail: enquiries@alberthotel.co.uk   web: www.alberthotel.co.uk
THE ALBERT HOTEL, MOUNTHOOLIE LANE, KIRKWALL, ORKNEY, KW15 1JZ

Visit the FHG website
www.holidayguides.com
for details of the wide choice of accommodation
featured in the full range of FHG titles

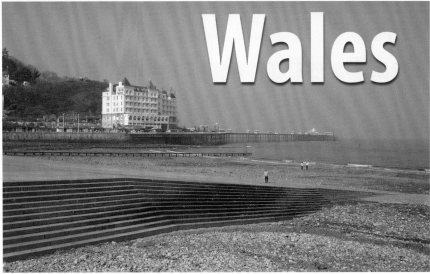

Llandudno, Anglesey & Gwynedd

SCENERY, history and the quality of life are the main ingredients of a holiday in Wales, which makes this a perfect destination for a holiday.

You can't go far in Wales without a view of mountains or the sea. And you can't go far in Wales without being in a National Park! Wales has three of these, each with its own special character. In the north, the Snowdonia National Park has mountains, moors, lakes and wooded valleys, dominated of course by Snowdon, the highest peak in England and Wales. At its northern edge is Anglesey and the North Wales Coast resorts, all popular tourist areas. But the atmosphere of the National Park is best experienced in the small towns and villages at its heart, such as Llanberis, Beddgelert, Betws-y-Coed and Capel Curig.

Approximately 100 km to the south and east is the Brecon Beacons National Park. From Llandeilo by the Black Mountain in the west, through the Brecon Beacons themselves to the Black Mountains and Hay-on-Wye on the border with England, here are grassy, smooth hills, open spaces, bare moors, lakes and forests. All that is lacking is the sea – and it's the sea which has made the Pembroke Coast National Park possible. From Tenby in the south to Cardigan in the north, the park offers every kind of coastal scenery: steep cliffs, sheltered bays and harbours, huge expanses of sand and shingle, rocky coves and quiet wooded inlets.

But 'scenery' doesn't end with the national parks. Wales also has five areas nominated officially as being of 'Outstanding Natural Beauty'. The Gower Peninsula, west of Swansea, is a scenic jewel – small but sparkling! The Wye Valley from Chepstow to Monmouth includes the ruined Tintern Abbey and many historic sites including Chepstow itself, Raglan and Caerleon.

The Isle of Anglesey, apart from its quiet beauty, claims the world's longest placename, usually shortened to Llanfair PG! The Llyn Peninsula, west of Snowdon is perhaps the most traditionally Welsh part of Wales and finally, the Clwydian Range behind Rhyl and Prestatyn, where St Asaph has the smallest cathedral in Britain.

www.visitwales.com

Wales
Great Days Out: Visits and Attractions

Henblas Country Park
Bodorgan, Anglesey • 01407 840440
Lots of fun for all the family - tractor tours, shearing demonstrations, indoor adventure playground, farm animals, crazy golf, tearoom.

Anglesey Sea Zoo
Brynsiencyn, Anglesey • 01248 430411
www.angleseyseazoo.co.uk
Meet the fascinating creatures that inhabit the sea and shores around Anglesey; adventure playground, shops and restaurant.

Ewe-phoria
Corwen, North Wales • 01490 460225
www.ewe-phoria.co.uk
Fascinating insight into the work of the shepherd and his sheepdog. Sheepdog and sheep shearing demonstrations, meet the lambs and puppies.

Sygun Copper Mine
Beddgelert, North Wales • 01766 890595
www.syguncoppermine.co.uk
Award-winning attraction with underground audio-visual tours. See stalagmites and stalactites formed from ferrous oxide.

Vale of Rheidol Railway
Aberystwyth, Ceredigion • 01970 625819
www.rheidolrailway.co.uk
An unforgettable journey by narrow gauge steam train, climbing over 600 feet in 12 miles from Aberystwyth to Devil's Bridge.There are many sharp turns and steep gradients, and the journey affords superb views of the valley.

Magic of Life Butterfly House
Aberystwyth, Ceredigion • 01970 880928
www.magicoflife.org
Hundreds of colourful butterflies, giant caterpillars and bizarre insects, plus collections of rare and endangered plants. Woodlands, walks and waterfalls nearby.

Folly Farm
Kilgetty, Pembrokeshire • 01834 812731
www.folly-farm.co.uk
In the heart of the countryside, with six fantastic zones - an award-winning attraction with a zoo, fungair, indoor/outdoor play areas and refreshments.

Manor House Wild Animal Park
Near Tenby, Pembrokeshire • 01646 651201
www.manorhousewildanimalpark.co.uk
Set in landscaped grounds round an 18th century manor. Lots of animals, including a 'close encounters' unit, plus daily falconry displays.

King Arthur's Labyrinth
Machynlleth, Powys • 01654 761584
www.kingarthurslabyrinth.com
Sail along an underground river deep into the Labyrinth and far into the past.... into a world of mystery, legends and storytelling. Tales of King Arthur and other ancient Welsh legends unfold in this dramatic underground setting.

Centre for Alternative Technology
Machynlleth, Powys • 01654 705950
www.cat.org.uk
World-renowned centre demonstrating practical and sustainable solutions to modern problems. Water-powered cliff railway, dynamic displays of wind and solar power, and organic gardens.

Rhondda Heritage Park
Trehafod, South Wales • 01443 682036
www.rhonddaheritagepark.com
One of the top heritage and cultural attractions in South Wales. The Black Gold Tour is guided by ex-miners and gives a vivid idea of what their working life was like.

Caldicot Castle & Country Park
Near Chepstow • 01291 420241
www.caldicotcastle.co.uk
Explore the castle's fascinating past with an audio tour, and take in the breathtaking views of the 55-acre grounds from the battlements. Children's activity centre, play area; tearoom.

BRYN BRAS CASTLE

Grade II* Listed Building

Llanrug, Near Caernarfon, Gwynedd LL55 4RE
Tel & Fax: (01286) 870210
e-mail: holidays@brynbrascastle.co.uk
www.brynbrascastle.co.uk

Enchanting Castle Apartments within a romantic Regency Castle of timeless charm, and a much-loved home. (Grade II* Listed Building of Architectural/Historic interest). Centrally situated in gentle Snowdonian foothills for enjoying North Wales' magnificent mountains, beaches, resorts, heritage and history. Many local restaurants and inns nearby. (Details available in our Information Room). A delightfully unique selection for 2-4 persons of fully self-contained, beautifully appointed, spacious, clean and peaceful accommodation, each with its own distinctive, individual character. Generously and graciously enhanced from antiques ... to dishwasher. 32 acres of truly tranquil landscaped gardens, sweeping lawns, woodland walks and panoramic hill-walk overlooking sea, Anglesey and Snowdon. The comfortable, warm and welcoming Castle in serene surroundings is open all year, including for short breaks, offering privacy and relaxation – ideal for couples. Regret children not accepted. Fully inclusive rents, including breakfast cereals etc., and much, much more...

Please contact Mrs Marita Gray-Parry directly any time for a brochure/booking
Self catering Apartments within the Castle
e.g. 2 persons for 2 nights from £195 incl "Romantic Breaks"
Inclusive Weekly Rents from £500

Anglesey & Gwynedd

Beautiful Victorian Country House standing in 20 acres of woodland, gardens and fields. High standard of accommodation in family, twin and double rooms, all en suite. Pets welcome. Stabling/grazing available.
Mrs Gwen McCreadie,

Deri Isaf

Dulas Bay, Isle of Anglesey LL70 9DX
Tel: 01248 410536 • Mobile: 07721 374471
e-mail: mccreadie@deriisaf.freeserve.co.uk
www.angleseyfarms.com/deri.htm

SILVER
ARIAN
ANGLESEY
TOURISM AWARDS
GWOBRAU TWRISTIAETH MÔN
2008
Best Bed & Breakfast

TREFEDDIAN HOTEL
ABERDOVEY, WALES
LL35 0SB
TEL 01654 767 213   WWW.TREFWALES.COM

Family friendly hotel in an idyllic location overlooking Cardigan Bay and near to the picturesque village of Aberdovey

Plenty of activities and attractions for all the family in the surrounding area

An ideal base to explore the many mountains and lakes of Snowdonia National Park

Award Winning Golden Sandy Beach at Aberdovey

Family Rooms
Baby Listening Service
Children's Supper Menu

Family friendly hotel
Indoor swimming pool
Lift to all floors
Indoor & Outdoor play areas
9 Hole Putting Green
Tennis Court
Beauty Salon

symbols

	Totally non-smoking		Pets Welcome
	Children Welcome		Christmas Breaks
	Suitable for Disabled Guests		Licensed

DOLSERAU HALL
COUNTRY HOUSE HOTEL

DOLSERAU HALL

This privately owned, friendly hotel lies in attractive grounds close to the river and is surrounded by green fields. The hotel's position offers the visitor peace & quiet, even in the high season. From the hotel, we have panoramic views over the surrounding pastures to the hills on either side of the valley. In the distance to the east are the Arran mountains and down the valley in the other direction, we look towards the Mawddach Estuary with Cadair Idris rising on the south side.

Essentially the hotel offers thoughtful personal service in relaxed traditional surroundings. It is a quiet hotel to which guests return, confident that they will find peace and relaxation.

The style is Country House, the atmosphere is calm and the service is personal. Comfort is a priority, with Egyptian cotton linen, Molton Brown toiletries and complementary afternoon tea and cake being just a few of the little luxuries one expects from a good country house hotel.

Sitting in 5 acres of its own, well established gardens, Dolserau Hall is half a mile from the nearest road (the lane that leads to our front drive is actually over a mile long). Guests are always impressed by the splendid isolation of this grand old house.

We look forward to welcoming you to our very own haven of peace in Southern Snowdonia.

Dolserau Hall Hotel
Dolgellau, Snowdonia LL40 2AG
Telephone: 01341 422522 • Fax: 01341 422400
E-mail: welcome@dolserau.co.uk
www.dolserau.co.uk

Bryn Gwyn Cottage
Llanberis, Anglesey & Gwynedd

Cosy cottage at the foot of Snowdon, sleeps five.
All modern conveniences. Ideal for mountains, lakes, rivers,
castles, horse riding, fishing, climbing, watersports,
beaches, golf, sailing; private guides. Pets welcome.
Contact Mr Eaton for details.

Tan-y-Coed
Llanrug, Caernarfon
Tel: 07887 790714

Talyllyn, Tywyn, Gwynedd LL36 9AJ

Gwesty Minffordd
Hotel

This 17th century Drovers' Inn offers today's traveller
all modern comforts. There is a mixture of old and
new style centrally
heated
bedrooms, and three lounges with log fires for
relaxation. The delicious meals on offer use local
Welsh produce, organic vegetables, Welsh
flavourings and are cooked on an Aga. With the
Cader Idris Path starting from the door, this Hotel is
ideal for walking, touring or sightseeing. The Talyllyn Lake,
Dolgoch Falls and the Centre for Alternative Technology are within five
miles. Further afield there are beaches and fishing ports, but whatever your
taste you will find a real welcome (or Croeso in Welsh) upon your return.
Perhaps that is why guests return year after year.

Tel: 01654 761665 Fax: 01654 761517
e-mail: hotel@minffordd.com • www.minffordd.com

Readers are requested to mention this FHG
guidebook when seeking accommodation

North Wales

Llanelli

Carmarthenshire

Ceredigion

Aberystwyth

Pembrokeshire

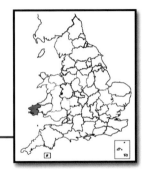

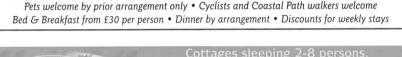

Whitland

Powys

Rhayader

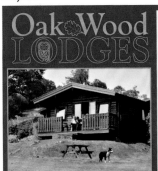
South Wales

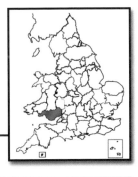

symbols

    Totally non-smoking

    Children Welcome

    Suitable for Disabled Guests

    Pets Welcome

    Christmas Breaks

    Licensed

Kylemore Abbey, Connemara

Photo courtesy PDPhoto.org

A LAND OF HISTORY AND HERITAGE, myths and magic, Ireland is easily accessible by plane or ferry, and ideal for a Short Break holiday at any time of year.

Northern Ireland's beauty is intertwined with tragic history, rich culture and the renowned friendliness of its people. The wild craggy mountains, splendid lakes and sweeping coastline make it an ideal playground for watersports enthusiasts, walkers, cyclists, hikers, rock climbers and sailors. But there are lots of things to keep those after a dose of culture enthralled, too. From oyster festivals to authentic horse fairs, and from ancient castles to elegant country houses, this spectacular part of Ireland is packed with things to do.

From the endless attractions of Dublin with its lively nightlife, museums and art galleries and, of course, its literary connection with Swift, Shaw, Yeats, Joyce and Beckett, to the charming west of Ireland where genuine hospitality is part of the culture, there are plenty of things to do and places to visit. The south-east area is steeped in history and boasts a heritage trail unrivalled by any other region in Ireland. Cork and Kerry to the south are perhaps the most attractive holiday areas, with a long coastline, mountains, many rivers and lakes. Some of Ireland's finest heritage attractions are to be found in the eastern coastal and midlands region, including prehistoric monuments, Celtic monasteries, castles, and grand houses and gardens. But it's not all about action. There's plenty of opportunity to relax; perhaps to enjoy a peaceful cruise on the waterways, or a chat with the locals in one of the friendly pubs and, best of all, to experience the warmest of warm welcomes wherever you go.

Tourism Ireland
0800 039 7000
www.discoverireland.com

Ireland

symbols

Totally non-smoking		Pets Welcome	
Children Welcome		Christmas Breaks	
Suitable for Disabled Guests		Licensed	

Ratings & Awards

For the first time ever the AA, VisitBritain, VisitScotland, and the Wales Tourist Board will use a single method of assessing and rating serviced accommodation. Irrespective of which organisation inspects an establishment the rating awarded will be the same, using a common set of standards, giving a clear guide of what to expect. The RAC is no longer operating an Hotel inspection and accreditation business.

Accommodation Standards: Star Grading Scheme

Using a scale of 1-5 stars the objective quality ratings give a clear indication of accommodation standard, cleanliness, ambience, hospitality, service and food, This shows the full range of standards suitable for every budget and preference, and allows visitors to distinguish between the quality of accommodation and facilities on offer in different establishments. All types of board and self-catering accommodation are covered, including hotels, B&Bs, holiday parks, campus accommodation, hostels, caravans and camping, and boats.

VisitBritain and the regional tourist boards, enjoyEngland.com, VisitScotland and VisitWales, and the AA have full details of the grading system on their websites

The more stars, the higher level of quality

★★★★★
exceptional quality, with a degree of luxury

★★★★
excellent standard throughout

★★★
very good level of quality and comfort

★★
good quality, well presented and well run

★
acceptable quality; simple, practical, no frills

National Accessible Scheme

If you have particular mobility, visual or hearing needs, look out for the National Accessible Scheme. You can be confident of finding accommodation or attractions that meet your needs by looking for the following symbols.

 Typically suitable for a person with sufficient mobility to climb a flight of steps but would benefit from fixtures and fittings to aid balance

 Typically suitable for a person with restricted walking ability and for those that may need to use a wheelchair some of the time and can negotiate a maximum of three steps

 Typically suitable for a person who depends on the use of a wheelchair and transfers unaided to and from the wheelchair in a seated position. This person may be an independent traveller

 Typically suitable for a person who depends on the use of a wheelchair in a seated position. This person also requires personal or mechanical assistance (eg carer, hoist).

Index of Towns and Counties

Other FHG titles for 2009

FHG Guides Ltd have a large range of attractive
oliday accommodation guides for all kinds of holiday opportunities throughout Britain.
They also make useful gifts at any time of year.
ur guides are available in most bookshops and larger newsagents but we will be happy
to post you a copy direct if you have any difficulty. POST FREE for addresses in the UK.
We will also post abroad but have to charge separately for post or freight.

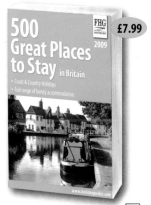

£7.99

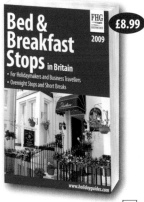

£8.99

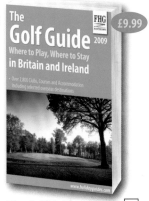

£9.99

500
Great Places to Stay
in Britain
• Coast & Country Holidays
• Full range of family
accommodation

Bed &
Breakfast Stops
in Britain
• For holidaymakers and business
travellers
• Overnight stops and Short
Breaks

The Golf Guide
Where to play, Where to stay.
• Over 2800 golf courses in Britain
with convenient accommodation.
• Holiday Golf in France, Portugal,
Spain, USA and Thailand.

£9.99

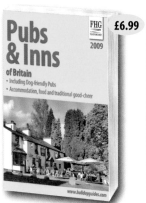

£6.99

£7.99

The Original
Pets Welcome!
• The bestselling guide to holidays
for pets and their owners

Pubs & Inns
of Britain
• Including Dog-friendly Pubs
• Accommodation, food and
traditional good cheer

Caravan
& Camping Holidays
in Britain
• Campsites and Caravan parks
• Facilities fully listed

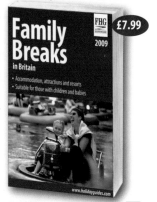

Family Breaks ☐
in Britain
• Accommodation, attractions and resorts
• Suitable for those with children and babies

Self-Catering Holidays ☐
in Britain
• Cottages, farms, apartments and chalets
• Over 400 places to stay

Country Hotels ☐
of Britain
• Hotels with Conference, Leisure and Wedding Facilities

Tick your choice above and send your order and payment to

**FHG Guides Ltd. Abbey Mill Business Centre
Seedhill, Paisley, Scotland PA1 1TJ
TEL: 0141- 887 0428 • FAX: 0141- 889 7204
e-mail: admin@fhguides.co.uk**

Deduct 10% for 2/3 titles or copies; 20% for 4 or more.

Send to: NAME ....

            ADDRESS ....

            ....

            ....

            POST CODE ....

I enclose Cheque/Postal Order for £ ....

            SIGNATURE ....DATE ....

Please complete the following to help us improve the service we provide.
How did you find out about our guides?:

☐ Press   ☐ Magazines   ☐ TV/Radio   ☐ Family/Friend   ☐ Other